Disciples Together on the Road

Words of Pope Francis for Priests

Libreria Editrice Vaticana
United States Conference of Catholic Bishops
Washington, DC

Cover Image, © Paul Haring/CNS.

First printing, October 2016

ISBN 978-1-60137-552-0

Contents

Introduction

A nine-year old boy:

My name is Julius. . . . My question is: What do you like best about being Pope?

Pope Francis:

The answer is simple. What I like is. . . . If I were to ask you what you like most about a meal, you would say cake, the dessert! Wouldn't you? But you have to eat everything. Quite honestly what I like is being a pastor, being a parish priest. I do not like office work. I don't like these tasks. I don't like giving official interviews—this one is not official, it's comfortable!—but I have to give them. Thus, what do I like best? Being a parish priest. Once, when I was rector of the faculty of theology, I was a priest in the parish next to the faculty, and you know, I liked teaching the Catechism to the children and saying Mass on Sunday with the children. There were 250 children, more or less; it was difficult for all of them to keep quiet, it was difficult. Dialoguing with children . . . I like this. You are a child and perhaps you will understand me. You are concrete, you do not ask theoretical, far-fetched questions: "Why is this so? Because . . ." It is just that I like being a parish priest and, as a priest what I like best is being with children, talking with them, and one learns so much. One learns so much.

I like being Pope in the style of a parish priest. Service. I like it in the sense that I feel good, when I visit the sick, when I talk with people who are somewhat in despair, sad. I really love going to prisons, but not those that put me in jail! To talk with the inmates . . . Perhaps you will understand what I am saying—every time I enter a prison, I ask myself: "Why them and not me?" And there I feel the salvation of Jesus Christ, the love of Jesus Christ for me. Because it is He who saved me. I am no less a sinner than they are, but the Lord took me by the hand. I feel this too. And when I go to a prison I am happy. Being Pope is being a bishop, being a priest, being a pastor. If a Pope is not a bishop, if a Pope is not a priest, if he is not a pastor, he may be a very intelligent, very important person, he may have a great deal of influence in society, but I think—I think!—that in his heart he is not happy. I don't know if I have responded to what you wanted to know.

(Pope Francis, Visit to the Evangelical Lutheran Church of Rome, November 15, 2015)

Julius's question and Pope Francis's response captures that Francis likes "being Pope in the style of a parish priest," "being a pastor."

It brings to mind the homily that the newly elected pope "from the ends of the earth" delivered just a fortnight after he appeared for the first time from the Loggia of St. Peter's Basilica. In it, he invited priests entrusted with the care of souls to be pastors with "the smell of the sheep" (March 28, 2013).

In a few essential words, the pontiff created a picture of the profile of the priest "after God's own heart." According to the pope, people "like it when the Gospel we preach touches their daily lives, when it runs down like the oil of Aaron to the edges of reality, when it brings light to moments of extreme darkness." Because of this, it is necessary that the priest comes out, first of all from himself, and reaches his flock wherever there is "suffering, bloodshed, blindness that longs for sight," wherever there are "prisoners in thrall to many evil masters."

In making this invitation to priests to go out into the world, the pope recalled that "it is not in soul-searching or constant introspection that we encounter the Lord." This is, in fact, likely to "minimize the power of grace, which comes alive and flourishes to the extent that we, in faith, go out and give ourselves and the Gospel to others, giving what little ointment we have to those who have nothing, nothing at all."

In response to little Julius and at the Chrism Mass later that year, Francis justifies his choice of "being" a pastor: Why? Because this gives him joy! And this brings to mind an iconic image of this pope, of the "Bergogliano pontificate"—the image of a smiling and joyful Francis holding a lamb on his shoulders (Visit to St. Alphonsus de Liguori Parish, Rome, January 6, 2014).

Pastors, then, with the joy and the love of God: Never be "sad priests." Whenever the pope speaks to an audience of priests, or refers to the ministerial priesthood in his speeches, he emphasizes the sadness that unfortunately he found in many men of God over the years—first as a Jesuit priest and then as bishop. Recently, meeting the participants in a conference organized by the Congregation for the Clergy, he said, "It is not normal that a priest is often sad, nervous or hard of character; it is not good and it does not do good, either for the priest or his people" (November 20, 2015). And he concluded, "We priests are apostles of joy, we proclaim the Gospel, that is the 'good news' par excellence." Pope Francis is convinced that "a priest who is a peaceful man will spread serenity around him, even in strenuous moments, conveying the beauty of the relationship with the Lord."

Undoubtedly pastoral service is often very tiring, and priests must be divided between multiple commitments, some not related to their mission but more suited to the work of public administration professionals. The pope gets it. He spoke of it at the Chrism Mass in 2015: "The tiredness of priests! Do you know how often I think about this weariness which all of you experience? I think about it and I pray about it, often, especially when I am tired myself. I pray for you as you labor amid the people of God, entrusted to your care, many of you in lonely and dangerous places." The knowledge that strengthens those who labor under such conditions, the pontiff recalled, is that "Our weariness, dear priests, is like incense which silently rises up to heaven. Our weariness goes straight to the heart of the Father."

This book brings together all the speeches and addresses that Pope Francis has given so far to priests and those in formation for the priesthood. It covers everything from the pope's homilies at the Chrism Mass to his remarks to diocesan priests during apostolic visitations; from his speeches to the Roman Curia to those delivered to the bishops during their *ad limina* visits; from his pronouncements after the *Angelus* to talks given to the Congregations for Bishops and for the Clergy; from the discourses on the formation of seminarians to words addressed to victims of sexual abuse by priests.

The excerpts in this book are not always given in full. Effort was made to limit the passages to when the pope discussed the theme of the gathering. The headings, if not already present, have been added for this publication.

Through his words, Pope Francis reminds every priest that he must continue to feel like the disciple on the road, all his life. The priest is to be aware that "sometimes we proceed with celerity, at other times our step is hesitant, we stop and we may even fall, but always staying on the path" (Address to the Congregation for the Clergy, October 3, 2014).

It is a road that, in this Holy Year, is for every priest a pilgrimage under the merciful gaze of the Supreme Pastor.

Chrism Mass

With the Odor of the Sheep

Vatican Basilica, Holy Thursday,
March 28, 2013

Dear Brothers and Sisters,

This morning I have the joy of celebrating my first Chrism Mass as the Bishop of Rome. I greet all of you with affection, especially you, dear priests, who, like myself, today recall the day of your ordination.

The readings and the Psalm of our Mass speak of God's "anointed ones": the suffering Servant of Isaiah, King David and Jesus our Lord. All three have this in common: the anointing that they receive is meant in turn to anoint God's faithful people, whose servants they are; they are anointed for the poor, for prisoners, for the oppressed. . . . A fine image of this "being for" others can be found in the Psalm 133: "It is like the precious oil upon the head, running down upon the beard, on the beard of Aaron, running down upon the collar of his robe" (v. 2). The image of spreading oil, flowing down from the beard of Aaron upon the collar of his sacred robe, is an image of the priestly anointing which, through Christ, the Anointed One, reaches the ends of the earth, represented by the robe.

The sacred robes of the High Priest are rich in symbolism. One such symbol is that the names of the children of Israel were engraved on the onyx stones mounted on the shoulder-pieces of the ephod, the ancestor of our present-day chasuble: six on the stone of the right shoulder-piece and six on that of the left (cf. Ex 28:6-14). The names of the twelve tribes of Israel were also engraved on the breastplate (cf. Ex 28:21). This means that the priest celebrates by carrying on his shoulders the people entrusted to his care and bearing their names written in his heart. When we put on our simple chasuble, it might well make us feel, upon our shoulders and in our hearts, the burdens and the faces of our faithful people, our saints and martyrs who are numerous in these times.

From the beauty of all these liturgical things, which is not so much about trappings and fine fabrics than about the glory of our God resplendent in his people, alive and strengthened, we turn now to a consideration of activity, action. The precious oil which anoints the head of Aaron does more than simply lend fragrance to his person; it overflows down to "the edges." The Lord will say this clearly: his anointing is meant for the poor, prisoners and the sick, for those who are sorrowing and alone. My dear brothers, the ointment is not intended just to make us fragrant, much less to be kept in a jar, for then it would become rancid . . . and the heart bitter.

A good priest can be recognized by the way his people are anointed: this is a clear proof. When our people are anointed with the oil of gladness, it is obvious: for example, when they leave Mass looking as if they have heard good news. Our people like to hear the Gospel preached with "unction," they like it when the Gospel we preach touches their daily lives, when it runs down like the oil of Aaron to the edges of reality, when it brings light to moments of extreme darkness, to the "outskirts" where people of faith are most exposed to the onslaught of those who want to tear down their faith. People thank us because they feel that we have prayed over the realities of their everyday lives, their troubles, their joys, their burdens and their hopes. And when they feel that the fragrance of the Anointed One, of Christ, has come to them through us, they feel encouraged to entrust to us everything they want to bring before the Lord: "Pray for me, Father, because I have this problem," "Bless me Father," "Pray for me"—these words are the sign that the anointing has flowed down to the edges of the robe, for it has turned into a prayer of supplication, the supplication of the People of God. When we have this relationship with God and with his people, and grace passes through us, then we are priests, mediators between God and men. What I want to emphasize is that we need constantly to stir up God's grace and perceive in every request, even those requests that are inconvenient and at times purely material or downright banal—but only apparently so— the desire of our people to be anointed with fragrant oil, since they know that we have it. To perceive and to sense, even as the Lord sensed the hope-filled anguish of the woman suffering from hemorrhages when she touched the hem of his garment. At that moment, Jesus, surrounded by people on every side, embodies all the beauty of Aaron vested in priestly raiment, with the oil running down upon his robes. It is a hidden beauty, one which shines forth only for those faith-filled eyes of the woman troubled with an issue of blood. But not even the disciples—future priests—see or understand: on the "existential outskirts," they see only what is on the surface: the crowd pressing in on Jesus from all sides (cf. Lk 8:42). The Lord, on the other hand, feels the power of the divine anointing which runs down to the edge of his cloak.

We need to "go out," then, in order to experience our own anointing, its power and its redemptive efficacy: to the "outskirts" where there is suffering, bloodshed, blindness that longs for sight, and prisoners in thrall to many evil masters. It is not in soul-searching or constant introspection that we encounter the Lord: self-help courses can be useful in life, but to live our priestly life going from one course to another, from one method to another, leads us to become pelagians and to minimize the power of grace, which comes alive and flourishes to the extent that we, in faith, go out and give ourselves and the Gospel to others, giving what little ointment we have to those who have nothing, nothing at all.

The priest who seldom goes out of himself, who anoints little—I won't say "not at all" because, thank God, the people take the oil from us anyway—misses out on the best of our people, on what can stir the depths of his priestly heart. Those who do not go out of themselves, instead of being mediators, gradually become intermediaries, managers. We know the difference: the intermediary, the manager, "has already received his reward," and since he doesn't put his own skin and his own heart on the line, he never hears a warm, heartfelt word of thanks. This is precisely the reason for the dissatisfaction of some, who end up sad— sad priests—in some sense becoming collectors of antiques or novelties, instead of being shepherds living with "the odor of the sheep." This I ask you: be shepherds, with the "odor of the sheep," make it real, as shepherds among your flock, fishers of men. True enough, the so-called crisis of priestly identity threatens us all and adds to the broader cultural crisis; but if we can resist its onslaught, we will be able to put out in the name of the Lord and cast our nets. It is not a bad thing that reality itself forces us to "put out into the deep," where what we are by grace is clearly seen as pure grace, out into the deep of the contemporary world, where the only thing that counts is "unction"—not function—and the nets which overflow with fish are those cast solely in the name of the One in whom we have put our trust: Jesus.

Dear lay faithful, be close to your priests with affection and with your prayers, that they may always be shepherds according to God's heart.

5

Dear priests, may God the Father renew in us the Spirit of holiness with whom we have been anointed. May he renew his Spirit in our hearts, that this anointing may spread to everyone, even to those "outskirts" where our faithful people most look for it and most appreciate it. May our people sense that we are the Lord's disciples; may they feel that their names are written upon our priestly vestments and that we seek no other identity; and may they receive through our words and deeds the oil of gladness which Jesus, the Anointed One, came to bring us. Amen.

Anointed with the Oil of Gladness

Vatican Basilica, Holy Thursday,
April 17, 2014

Dear Brother Priests,

In the eternal "today" of Holy Thursday, when Christ showed his love for us to the end (cf. Jn 13:1), we recall the happy day of the institution of the priesthood, as well as the day of our own priestly ordination. The Lord anointed us in Christ with the oil of gladness, and this anointing invites us to accept and appreciate this great gift: the gladness, the joy of being a priest. Priestly joy is a priceless treasure, not only for the priest himself but for the entire faithful people of God: that faithful people from which he is called to be anointed and which he, in turn, is sent to anoint.

Anointed with the oil of gladness so as to anoint others with the oil of gladness. Priestly joy has its source in the Father's love, and the Lord wishes the joy of this Love to be "ours" and to be "complete" (Jn 15:11). I like to reflect on joy by contemplating Our Lady, for Mary, the "Mother of the living Gospel, is a wellspring of joy for God's little ones" (*Evangelii Gaudium*, no. 288). I do not think it is an exaggeration to say that priest is very little indeed: the incomparable grandeur of the gift granted us for the ministry sets us among the least of men. The priest is the poorest of men unless Jesus enriches him by his poverty, the most useless of servants unless Jesus calls him his friend, the most ignorant of men unless Jesus patiently teaches him as he did Peter, the frailest of Christians unless the Good Shepherd strengthens him in the midst of the flock. No one is more "little" than a priest left to his own devices; and so our prayer of protection against every snare of the Evil One is the prayer of our Mother: I am a priest because he has regarded my littleness (cf. Lk 1:48). And in that littleness we find our joy. Joy in our littleness!

For me, there are three significant features of our priestly joy. It is a joy which *anoints us* (not one which "greases" us, making us unctuous, sumptuous and presumptuous), it is a joy which is *imperishable* and it is a *missionary* joy which spreads and attracts, starting backwards—with those farthest away from us.

A joy which anoints us. In a word: it has penetrated deep within our hearts, it has shaped them and strengthened them sacramentally. The signs of the ordination liturgy speak to us of the Church's maternal desire to pass on and share with others all that the Lord has given us: the laying on of hands, the anointing with sacred chrism, the clothing with sacred vestments, the first consecration which immediately follows. . . . Grace fills us to the brim and overflows, fully, abundantly and entirely in each priest. We are anointed down to our very bones . . . and our joy, which wells up from deep within, is the echo of this anointing.

An imperishable joy. The fullness of the Gift, which no one can take away or increase, is an unfailing source of joy: an imperishable joy which the Lord has promised no one can take from us (Jn 16:22). It can lie dormant, or be clogged by sin or by life's troubles, yet deep down it remains intact, like the embers of a burnt log beneath the ashes, and it can always be renewed. Paul's exhortation to Timothy remains ever timely: I remind you to fan into flame the gift of God that is within you through the laying on of my hands (cf. 2 Tm 1:6).

A missionary joy. I would like especially to share with you and to stress this third feature: priestly joy is deeply bound up with God's holy and faithful people, for it is an eminently missionary joy. Our anointing is meant for anointing God's holy and faithful people: for baptizing and confirming them, healing and sanctifying them, blessing, comforting and evangelizing them.

And since this joy is one which only springs up when the shepherd is in the midst of his flock (for even in the silence of his prayer, the shepherd who worships the Father is with his sheep), it is a "guarded joy," watched over by the flock itself. Even in those gloomy moments when everything looks dark and a feeling of isolation takes hold of us, in those moments of listlessness and boredom which at times overcome us in our priestly life (and which I too have experienced), even in those moments God's people are able to "guard" that joy; they are able to protect you, to embrace you and to help you open your heart to find renewed joy.

A "guarded joy": one guarded by the flock but also guarded by three sisters who surround it, tend it and defend it: sister poverty, sister fidelity and sister obedience.

The joy of priests is a joy which is sister to poverty. The priest is poor in terms of purely human joy. He has given up so much! And because he is poor, he, who gives so much to others, has to seek his joy from the Lord and from God's faithful people. He doesn't need to try to create it for himself. We know that our people are very generous in thanking priests for their slightest blessing and especially for the sacraments. Many people, in speaking of the crisis of priestly identity, fail to realize that identity presupposes belonging. There is no identity—and consequently joy of life—without an active and unwavering sense of belonging to God's faithful people (cf. *Evangelii Gaudium*, no. 268). The priest who tries to find his priestly identity by soul-searching and introspection may well encounter nothing more than "exit" signs, signs that say: exit from yourself, exit to seek God in adoration, go out and give your people what was entrusted to you, for your people will make you feel and taste who you are, what your name is, what your identity is, and they will make you rejoice in that hundredfold which the Lord has promised to those who serve him. Unless you "exit" from yourself, the oil grows rancid and the anointing cannot be fruitful. Going out from ourselves presupposes self-denial; it means poverty.

Priestly joy is a joy which is sister to fidelity. Not primarily in the sense that we are all "immaculate" (would that by God's grace we were!), for we are sinners, but in the sense of an ever renewed fidelity to the one Bride, to the Church. Here fruitfulness is key. The spiritual children which the Lord gives each priest, the children he has baptized, the families he has blessed and helped on their way, the sick he has comforted, the young people he catechizes and helps to grow, the poor he assists . . . all these are the "Bride" whom he rejoices to treat as his supreme and only love and to whom he is constantly faithful. It is the living Church, with a first name and a last name, which the priest shepherds in his parish or in the mission entrusted to him. That mission brings him joy whenever he is faithful to it, whenever he does all that he has to do and lets go of everything that he has to let go of, as long as he stands firm amid the flock which the Lord has entrusted to him: Feed my sheep (cf. Jn 21:16, 17).

Priestly joy is a joy which is sister to obedience. An obedience to the Church in the hierarchy which gives us, as it were, not simply the external framework for our obedience: the parish to which I am sent, my ministerial assignments, my particular work . . . but also union with God the Father, the source of all fatherhood. It is likewise an obedience to the Church in service: in availability and readiness to serve everyone, always and as best I can, following the example of "Our Lady of Promptness" (cf. Lk 1:39, *meta spoudes*), who hastens to serve Elizabeth her kinswoman and is concerned for the kitchen of Cana when the wine runs out. The availability of her priests makes the Church a house with open doors, a refuge for sinners, a home for people living on the streets, a place of loving care for the sick, a camp for the young, a classroom for catechizing children about to make their First Communion. . . . Wherever God's people have desires or needs, there is the priest, who knows how to listen (*ob-audire*) and feels a loving mandate from Christ who sends him to relieve that need with mercy or to encourage those good desires with resourceful charity.

All who are called should know that genuine and complete joy does exist in this world: it is the joy of being taken from the people we love and then being sent back to them as dispensers of the gifts and counsels of Jesus, the one Good Shepherd who, with deep compassion for all the little ones and the outcasts of this earth, wearied and oppressed like sheep without a shepherd, wants to associate many others to his ministry, so as himself to remain with us and to work, in the person of his priests, for the good of his people.

On this Holy Thursday, I ask the Lord Jesus to enable many young people to discover that burning zeal which joy kindles in our hearts as soon as we have the stroke of boldness needed to respond willingly to his call.

On this Holy Thursday, I ask the Lord Jesus to preserve the joy sparkling in the eyes of the recently ordained who go forth to devour the world, to spend themselves fully in the midst of God's faithful people, rejoicing as they prepare their first homily, their first Mass, their first Baptism, their first confession. . . . It is the joy of being able to share with wonder, and for the first time as God's anointed, the treasure of the Gospel and to feel the faithful people anointing you again and in yet another way: by their requests, by bowing their heads for your blessing, by taking your hands, by bringing you their children, by pleading for their sick. . . . Preserve, Lord, in your young priests the joy of going forth, of doing everything as if for the first time, the joy of spending their lives fully for you.

On this Thursday of the priesthood, I ask the Lord Jesus to confirm the priestly joy of those who have already ministered for some years.

The joy which, without leaving their eyes, is also found on the shoulders of those who bear the burden of the ministry, those priests who, having experienced the labors of the apostolate, gather their strength and rearm themselves: "get a second wind," as the athletes say. Lord, preserve the depth, wisdom and maturity of the joy felt by these older priests. May they be able to pray with Nehemiah: "The joy of the Lord is my strength" (cf. Neh 8:10).

Finally, on this Thursday of the priesthood, I ask the Lord Jesus to make better known the joy of elderly priests, whether healthy or infirm. It is the joy of the Cross, which springs from the knowledge that we possess an imperishable treasure in perishable earthen vessels. May these priests find happiness wherever they are; may they experience already, in the passage of the years, a taste of eternity (Guardini). May they know, Lord, the joy of handing on the torch, the joy of seeing new generations of their spiritual children, and of hailing the promises from afar, smiling and at peace, in that hope which does not disappoint.

The Tiredness of Priests

Vatican Basilica, Holy Thursday,
April 2, 2015

"My hand shall ever abide with him, my arms also shall strengthen him" (Ps 89:21).

This is what the Lord means when he says: "I have found David, my servant; with my holy oil I have anointed him" (v. 20). It is also what our Father thinks whenever he "encounters" a priest. And he goes on to say: "My faithfulness and my steadfast love shall be with him. . . . He shall cry to me, 'You are my Father, my God and the rock of my salvation'" (vv. 24, 26).

It is good to enter with the Psalmist into this monologue of our God. He is talking about us, his priests, his pastors. But it is not really a monologue, since he is not the only one speaking. The Father says to Jesus: "Your friends, those who love you, can say to me in a particular way: 'You are my Father'" (cf. Jn 14:21). If the Lord is so concerned about helping us, it is because he knows that the task of anointing his faithful people is not easy, it is demanding; it can tire us. We experience this in so many ways: from the ordinary fatigue brought on by our daily apostolate to the weariness of sickness, death and even martyrdom.

The tiredness of priests! Do you know how often I think about this weariness which all of you experience? I think about it and I pray about it, often, especially when I am tired myself. I pray for you as you labor amid the people of God entrusted to your care, many of you in lonely and dangerous places. Our weariness, dear priests, is like incense which silently rises up to heaven (cf. Ps 141:2; Rev 8:3-4). Our weariness goes straight to the heart of the Father.

Know that the Blessed Virgin Mary is well aware of this tiredness and she brings it straight to the Lord. As our Mother, she knows when her children are weary, and this is her greatest concern. "Welcome! Rest, my child. We will speak afterwards . . ." "Whenever we draw near to her, she says to us: "Am I not here with you, I who am your Mother?" (cf.

Evangelii Gaudium, no. 286). And to her Son she will say, as she did at Cana, "They have no wine" (Jn 2:3).

It can also happen that, whenever we feel weighed down by pastoral work, we can be tempted to rest however we please, as if rest were not itself a gift of God. We must not fall into this temptation. Our weariness is precious in the eyes of Jesus who embraces us and lifts us up. "Come to me, all who labor and are overburdened, and I will give you rest" (Mt 11:28). Whenever a priest feels dead tired, yet is able to bow down in adoration and say: "Enough for today Lord," and entrust himself to the Father, he knows that he will not fall but be renewed. The one who anoints God's faithful people with oil is also himself anointed by the Lord: "He gives you a garland instead of ashes, the oil of gladness instead of mourning, the mantle of praise instead of a faint spirit" (cf. Is 61:3).

Let us never forget that a key to fruitful priestly ministry lies in how we rest and in how we look at the way the Lord deals with our weariness. How difficult it is to learn how to rest! This says much about our trust and our ability to realize that we too are sheep: we need the help of the Shepherd. A few questions can help us in this regard.

Do I know how to rest by accepting the love, gratitude and affection which I receive from God's faithful people? Or, once my pastoral work is done, do I seek more refined relaxations, not those of the poor but those provided by a consumerist society? Is the Holy Spirit truly "rest in times of weariness" for me, or is he just someone who keeps me busy? Do I know how to seek help from a wise priest? Do I know how to take a break from myself, from the demands I make on myself, from my self-seeking and from my self-absorption? Do I know how to spend time with Jesus, with the Father, with the Virgin Mary and St. Joseph, with my patron saints, and to find rest in their demands, which are easy and light, and in their pleasures, for they delight to be in my company, and in their concerns and standards, which have only to do with the greater glory of God? Do I know how to rest from my enemies under the Lord's protection? Am I preoccupied with how I should speak and act, or do I entrust myself to the Holy Spirit, who will teach me what I need to say in every situation? Do I worry needlessly, or, like Paul, do I find repose by saying: "I know him in whom I have placed my trust" (2 Tm 1:12)?

Let us return for a moment to what today's liturgy describes as the work of the priest: to bring good news to the poor, to proclaim freedom to prisoners and healing to the blind, to offer liberation to the downtrodden and to announce the year of the Lord's favor. Isaiah also mentions consoling the broken-hearted and comforting the afflicted.

These are not easy or purely mechanical jobs, like running an office, building a parish hall or laying out a soccer field for the young of the parish. . . . The tasks of which Jesus speaks call for the ability to show compassion; our hearts are to be "moved" and fully engaged in carrying them out. We are to rejoice with couples who marry; we are to laugh with the children brought to the baptismal font; we are to accompany young fiancés and families; we are to suffer with those who receive the anointing of the sick in their hospital beds; we are to mourn with those burying a loved one. . . . All these emotions . . . if we do not have an open heart, can exhaust the heart of a shepherd. For us priests, what happens in the lives of our people is not like a news bulletin: we know our people, we sense what is going on in their hearts. Our own heart, sharing in their suffering, feels "compassion," is exhausted, broken into a thousand pieces, moved and even "consumed" by the people. Take this, eat this. . . . These are the words the priest of Jesus whispers repeatedly while caring for his faithful people: Take this, eat this; take this, drink this. . . . In this way our priestly life is given over in service, in closeness to the People of God . . . and this always leaves us weary.

I wish to share with you some forms of weariness on which I have meditated.

There is what we can call "the weariness of people, the weariness of the crowd." For the Lord, and for us, this can be exhausting—so the Gospel tells us—yet it is a good weariness, a fruitful and joyful exhaustion. The people who followed Jesus, the families which brought their children to him to be blessed, those who had been cured, those who came with their friends, the young people who were so excited about the Master . . . they did not even leave him time to eat. But the Lord never tired of being with people. On the contrary, he seemed renewed by their presence (cf. *Evangelii Gaudium*, no. 11). This weariness in the midst of activity is a grace on which all priests can draw (cf. ibid., no. 279). And how beautiful it is! People love their priests, they want and need their shepherds! The faithful never leave us without something to do, unless we hide in our offices or go out in our cars wearing sunglasses. There is a good and healthy tiredness. It is the exhaustion of the priest who wears the smell of the sheep . . . but also smiles the smile of a father rejoicing in his children or grandchildren. It has nothing to do with those who wear expensive cologne and who look at others from afar and from above (cf. ibid., no. 97). We are the friends of the Bridegroom: this is our joy. If Jesus is shepherding the flock in our midst, we cannot be shepherds who are glum, plaintive or, even worse, bored. The smell of the sheep and the smile of a father. . . . Weary, yes, but with the joy of those who hear the Lord saying: "Come, O blessed of my Father" (Mt 25:34).

There is also the kind of weariness which we can call "the weariness of enemies." The devil and his minions never sleep and, since their ears cannot bear to hear the word of God, they work tirelessly to silence that word and to distort it. Confronting them is more wearying. It involves not only doing good, with all the exertion this entails, but also defending the flock and oneself from evil (cf. *Evangelii Gaudium*, no. 83). The evil one is far more astute than we are, and he is able to demolish in a moment what it took us years of patience to build up. Here we need to implore the grace to learn how to "offset" (and it is an important habit to acquire): to thwart evil without pulling up the good wheat, or presuming to protect like supermen what the Lord alone can protect. All this helps us not to let our guard down before the depths of iniquity, before the mockery of the wicked. In these situations of weariness, the Lord says to us: "Have courage! I have overcome the world!" (Jn 16:33). The word of God gives us strength.

And finally—I say finally lest you be too wearied by this homily itself!—there is also "weariness of ourselves" (cf. *Evangelii Gaudium*, no. 277). This may be the most dangerous weariness of all. That is because the other two kinds come from being exposed, from going out of ourselves to anoint and to do battle (for our job is to care for others). But this third kind of weariness is more "self-referential": it is dissatisfaction with oneself, but not the dissatisfaction of someone who directly confronts himself and serenely acknowledges his sinfulness and his need for God's mercy, his help; such people ask for help and then move forward. Here we are speaking of a weariness associated with "wanting yet not wanting," having given up everything but continuing to yearn for the fleshpots of Egypt, toying with the illusion of being something different. I like to call this kind of weariness "flirting with spiritual worldliness." When we are alone, we realize how many areas of our life are steeped in this worldliness, so much so that we may feel that it can never be completely washed away. This can be a dangerous kind of weariness. The Book of Revelation shows us the reason for this weariness: "You have borne up for my sake and you have not grown weary. But I have this against you, that you have abandoned the love you had at first" (Rev 2:3-4). Only love gives true rest. What is not loved becomes tiresome, and in time, brings about a harmful weariness.

The most profound and mysterious image of how the Lord deals with our pastoral tiredness is that, "having loved his own, he loved them to the end" (Jn 13:1): the scene of his washing the feet of his disciples. I like to think of this as the *cleansing of discipleship*. The Lord purifies the path of discipleship itself. He "gets involved" with us (*Evangelii Gaudium*, no. 24), becomes personally responsible for removing every stain, all that grimy, worldly smog which clings to us from the journey we make in his name.

From our feet, we can tell how the rest of our body is doing. The way we follow the Lord reveals how our heart is faring. The wounds on our feet, our sprains and our weariness, are signs of how we have followed him, of the paths we have taken in seeking the lost sheep and in leading the flock to green pastures and still waters (cf. ibid., no. 270). The Lord washes us and cleanses us of all the dirt our feet have accumulated in following him. This is something holy. Do not let your feet remain dirty. Like battle wounds, the Lord kisses them and washes away the grime of our labors.

Our discipleship itself is cleansed by Jesus, so that we can rightly feel "joyful," "fulfilled," "free of fear and guilt," and impelled to go out "even to the ends of the earth, to every periphery." In this way we can bring the good news to the most abandoned, knowing that "he is with us always, even to the end of the world." And please, let us ask for the grace to learn how to be weary, but weary in the best of ways!

Witnesses to and Ministers of Mercy

Vatican Basilica, Holy Thursday,
March 24, 2016

After hearing Jesus read from the Prophet Isaiah and say: "Today this Scripture has been fulfilled in your hearing" (Lk 4:21), the congregation in the synagogue of Nazareth might well have burst into applause. They might have then wept for joy, as did the people when Nehemiah and Ezra the priest read from the book of the Law found while they were rebuilding the walls. But the Gospels tell us that Jesus' townspeople did the opposite; they closed their hearts to him and sent him off. At first, "all spoke well of him, and wondered at the gracious words that came from his mouth" (4:22). But then an insidious question began to make the rounds: "Is this not the son of Joseph, the carpenter?" (4:22). And then, "they were filled with rage" (4:28). They wanted to throw him off the cliff. This was in fulfillment of the elderly Simeon's prophecy to the Virgin Mary that he would be "a sign of contradiction" (2:34). By his words and actions, Jesus lays bare the secrets of the heart of every man and woman.

Where the Lord proclaims the Gospel of the Father's unconditional mercy to the poor, the outcast and the oppressed, is the very place we are called to take a stand, to "fight the good fight of the faith" (1 Tm 6:12). His battle is not against men and women, but against the devil (cf. Eph 6:12), the enemy of humanity. But the Lord "passes through the midst" of all those who would stop him and "continues on his way" (Lk 4:30). Jesus does not fight to build power. If he breaks down walls and challenges our sense of security, he does this to open the floodgates of that mercy which, with the Father and the Holy Spirit, he wants to pour out upon our world. A mercy which expands; it proclaims and brings newness; it heals, liberates and proclaims the year of the Lord's favor.

The mercy of our God is infinite and indescribable. We express the power of this mystery as an "ever greater" mercy, a mercy in motion, a mercy that each day seeks to make progress, taking small steps forward and advancing in that wasteland where indifference and violence have predominated.

17

This was the way of the Good Samaritan, who "showed mercy" (cf. Lk 10:37): he was moved, he drew near to the wounded man, he bandaged his wounds, took him to the inn, stayed there that evening and promised to return and cover any further cost. This is the way of mercy, which gathers together small gestures. Without demeaning, it grows with each helpful sign and act of love. Every one of us, looking at our own lives as God does, can try to remember the ways in which the Lord has been merciful toward us, how he has been much more merciful than we imagined. In this we can find the courage to ask him to take a step further and to reveal yet more of his mercy in the future: "Show us, Lord, your mercy" (Ps 85:8). This paradoxical way of praying to an ever more merciful God, helps us to tear down those walls with which we try to contain the abundant greatness of his heart. It is good for us to break out of our set ways, because it is proper to the Heart of God to overflow with tenderness, with ever more to give. For the Lord prefers something to be wasted rather than one drop of mercy be held back. He would rather have many seeds be carried off by the birds of the air than have one seed be missing, since each of those seeds has the capacity to bear abundant fruit, thirtyfold, sixtyfold, even a hundredfold.

As priests, we are witnesses to and ministers of the ever-increasing abundance of the Father's mercy; we have the rewarding and consoling task of incarnating mercy, as Jesus did, who "went about doing good and healing" (Acts 10:38) in a thousand ways so that it could touch everyone. We can help to enculturate mercy, so that each person can embrace it and experience it personally. This will help all people truly understand and practice mercy with creativity, in ways that respect their local cultures and families.

Today, during this Holy Thursday of the Jubilee Year of Mercy, I would like to speak of two areas in which the Lord shows excess in mercy. Based on his example, we also should not hesitate in showing excess. The first area I am referring to is encounter; the second is God's forgiveness, which shames us while also giving us dignity.

The first area where we see *God showing excess* in his ever-increasing mercy is that of *encounter*. He gives himself completely and in such a way that every encounter leads to rejoicing. In the parable of the Merciful Father we are astounded by the man who runs, deeply moved, to his son, and throws his arms around him; we see how he embraces his son, kisses him, puts a ring on his finger, and then gives him his sandals, thus showing that he is a son and not a servant. Finally, he gives orders to everyone and organizes a party. In contemplating with awe this superabundance of the Father's joy that is freely and boundlessly expressed when his son returns, we should not be fearful of exaggerating our gratitude. Our attitude should be that of the poor leper who, seeing himself healed, leaves his nine friends who go off to do what Jesus ordered, and goes back to kneel at the feet of the Lord, glorifying and thanking God aloud.

Mercy restores everything; it restores dignity to each person. This is why effusive gratitude is the proper response: we have to go the party, to put on our best clothes, to cast off the rancor of the elder brother, to rejoice and give thanks. . . . Only in this way, participating fully in such rejoicing, is it possible to think straight, to ask for forgiveness, and see more clearly how to make up for the evil we have committed. It would be good for us to ask ourselves: After going to confession, do I rejoice? Or do I move on immediately to the next thing, as we would after going to the doctor, when we hear that the test results are not so bad and put them back in their envelope? And when I give alms, do I give time to the person who receives them to express their gratitude, do I celebrate the smile and the blessings that the poor offer, or do I continue on in haste with my own affairs after tossing in a coin?

The second area in which we see how *God exceeds* in his ever greater mercy is *forgiveness itself*. God does not only forgive incalculable debts, as he does to that servant who begs for mercy but is then miserly to his own debtor; he also enables us to move directly from the most shameful disgrace to the highest dignity without any intermediary stages. The Lords allows the forgiven woman to wash his feet with her tears. As soon as Simon confesses his sin and begs Jesus to send him away, the Lord raises him to be a fisher of men. We, however, tend to separate these two attitudes: when we are ashamed of our sins, we hide ourselves and walk around with our heads down, like Adam and Eve; and when we are raised up to some dignity, we try to cover up our sins and take pleasure in being seen, almost showing off.

Our response to God's superabundant forgiveness should be always to preserve *that healthy tension between a dignified shame and a shamed dignity*. It is the attitude of one who seeks a humble and lowly place, but who can also allow the Lord to raise him up for the good of the mission, without complacency. The model that the Gospel consecrates, and which can help us when we confess our sins, is Peter, who allowed himself to be questioned about his love for the Lord, but who also renewed his acceptance of the ministry of shepherding the flock which the Lord had entrusted to him.

To grow in this "dignity which is capable of humbling itself," and which delivers us from thinking that we are more or are less than what we are by grace, can help us understand the words of the prophet Isaiah that immediately follow the passage our Lord read in the synagogue at Nazareth: "You will be called priests of the Lord, ministers of our God" (Is 61:6). It is people who are poor, hungry, prisoners of war, without a future, cast to one side and rejected, that the Lord transforms into a priestly people.

As priests, we identify with people who are excluded, people the Lord saves. We remind ourselves that there are countless masses of people who are poor, uneducated, prisoners, who find themselves in such situations because others oppress them. But we too remember that each of us knows the extent to which we too are often blind, lacking the radiant light of faith, not because we do not have the Gospel close at hand, but because of an excess of complicated theology. We feel that our soul thirsts for spirituality, not for a lack of Living Water which we only sip from, but because of an excessive "bubbly" spirituality, a "light" spirituality. We feel ourselves also trapped, not so much by insurmountable stone walls or steel enclosures that affect many peoples, but rather by a digital, virtual worldliness that is opened and closed by a simple *click*. We are oppressed, not by threats and pressures, like so many poor people, but by the allure of a thousand commercial advertisements which we cannot shrug off to walk ahead, freely, along paths that lead us to love of our brothers and sisters, to the Lord's flock, to the sheep who wait for the voice of their shepherds.

Jesus comes to redeem us, to send us out, to transform us from being poor and blind, imprisoned and oppressed, to become ministers of mercy and consolation. He says to us, using the words the prophet Ezekiel spoke to the people who sold themselves and betrayed the Lord: "I will remember my covenant with you in the days of your youth. . . . Then you will remember your ways, and be ashamed when I take your sisters, both your elder and your younger, and give them to you as daughters, but not on account of the covenant with you. I will establish my covenant with you, and you shall know that I am the Lord, that you may remember and be confounded, and never open your mouth again because of your shame, when I forgive you all that you have done, says the Lord God" (Ez 16:60-63).

In this Jubilee Year we celebrate our Father with hearts full of gratitude, and we pray to him that "he remember his mercy forever"; let us receive, with a dignity that is able to humble itself, the mercy revealed in the wounded flesh of our Lord Jesus Christ. Let us ask him to cleanse us of all sin and free us from every evil. And with the grace of the Holy Spirit let us commit ourselves anew to bringing God's mercy to all men and women, and performing those works which the Spirit inspires in each of us for the common good of the entire People of God.

Meetings with Priests

A Preacher Who Does Not Prepare Is Not "Spiritual"

Evangelii Gaudium, *no. 145*

Preparation for preaching is so important a task that a prolonged time of study, prayer, reflection and pastoral creativity should be devoted to it. With great affection I wish to stop for a moment and offer a method of preparing homilies. Some may find these suggestions self-evident, but I consider it helpful to offer them as a way of emphasizing the need to devote quality time to this precious ministry. Some pastors argue that such preparation is not possible given the vast number of tasks which they must perform; nonetheless, I presume to ask that each week a sufficient portion of personal and community time be dedicated to this task, even if less time has to be given to other important activities. Trust in the Holy Spirit who is at work during the homily is not merely passive but active and creative. It demands that we offer ourselves and all our abilities as instruments (cf. Rom 12:1) which God can use. A preacher who does not prepare is not "spiritual"; he is dishonest and irresponsible with the gifts he has received.

A Priest of the Street

Words at the End of the Holy Mass in the
Parish of St. Anna in the Vatican

March 17, 2013

I want to introduce to you a priest who comes from far away, a priest who works with children and with drug addicts on the street. He opened a school for them; he has done many things to make Jesus known, and all those boys and girls off the street, they today work with the studies they have done; they have the ability to work, they believe and they love Jesus. I ask you Gonzalo, come greet the people: pray for him. He works in Uruguay; he is the founder of *Jubilar Juan Pablo II*. This is his work. I do not know how he came here, but I will find out! Thanks. Pray for him.

To Listen, to Walk, and to Proclaim Even to the Outskirts

Meeting with Clergy, Consecrated People and Members of Diocesan Pastoral Councils

Cathedral of San Rufino, Assisi, October 4, 2013

How needed pastoral councils are! A bishop cannot guide a diocese without pastoral councils. A parish priest cannot guide the parish without the parish council. . . .

Now, briefly, I would like to highlight several aspects of your life as a Community. . . .

1. The first thing is *to listen to God's Word*. I think we can all improve a bit in this respect: by becoming better listeners of the Word of God, in order to be less rich on our own words and richer in his words. I think of the priest who has the task of preaching. How can he preach if he has not first opened his heart, not listened in silence to the Word of God? Away with these never ending, boring homilies that no one understands. . . .

2. The second aspect is *walking*. . . . Here I think once more of you priests, and let me place myself in your company. What could be more beautiful for us than walking with our people? It is beautiful! When I think of the parish priests who knew the names of their parishioners, who went to visit them; even as one of them told me: "I know the name of each family's dog." They even knew the dog's name! How nice it was! What could be more beautiful than this? I repeat it often: walking with our people, sometimes in front, sometimes in the middle, and sometimes behind: in front in order to guide the community, in the middle in order to encourage and support; and at the back in order to keep it united and so that no one lags too, too far behind, to keep them united. There is another reason too: because the people have a "nose"! The people scent out, discover, new ways to walk, it has the "*sensus fidei*," as theologians call it. What could be more beautiful than this?

3. Therefore: to listen, to walk, and the third aspect is missionary: *to proclaim even to the outskirts*. . . . I wish to emphasize it, because it is something I also experienced a great deal when I was in Buenos Aires: the importance of going out to meet the other in the outskirts, which are places, but which are primarily people living in particular situations in life. This was true in my former diocese, that of Buenos Aires. The outskirt which hurt me a great deal was to find children in middle class families who didn't know how to make the Sign of the Cross. But you see, this is an outskirt! And I ask you, here in this diocese, are there children who do not know how to make the Sign of the Cross? Think about it. These are true outskirts of existence where God is absent.

In one sense, the outskirts of this diocese, for example, are the areas of the diocese that risk being left on the margins, beyond the street lights. But they are also people and human realities that are marginalized and despised. They are people who perhaps live physically close to the "center" but who spiritually are very far away.

Do not be afraid to go out and meet these people and situations. Do not allow yourselves to be impeded by prejudice, by habit, by an intellectual or pastoral rigidity, by the famous "we've always done it this way!" However, we can only go to the outskirts if we carry the Word of God in our hearts and if we walk with the Church, like St. Francis. Otherwise, we take ourselves, not the Word of God, and this isn't good, it doesn't help anyone! We are not the ones who save the world: it is the Lord himself who saves it!

There you are, dear friends. I haven't given you any new recipes. I don't have any, and don't believe anyone who says he does: they don't exist. However, I did find several beautiful and important aspects of the journey of your Church that should be developed, and I want to confirm you in these. Listen to the Word, walk together as brothers and sisters, proclaim the Gospel to the outskirts! May the Lord bless you, may Our Lady protect you, and may St. Francis help you all to experience the joy of being disciples of the Lord! Thank you.

The Priest Is a Man of Mercy and Compassion

Meeting with the Parish Priests of Rome
Paul VI Hall, March 6, 2014

When together with the Cardinal Vicar, we planned this meeting, I told him that I could offer you a meditation on the theme of mercy. At the beginning of Lent, it does us good to reflect together as priests on mercy. We all need it. Also the faithful, since as pastors we must extend great, great mercy!

The passage from the Gospel of Matthew that we heard makes us turn our gaze to Jesus as he goes about the cities and villages. And this is curious. Where was Jesus most often, where could he most easily be found? On the road. He might have seemed to be homeless, because he was always on the road. Jesus' life was on the road. He especially invites us to grasp the depths of his heart, what he feels for the crowds, for the people he encounters: that interior attitude of "compassion"; seeing the crowds, he felt compassion for them. For he saw the people were "harassed and helpless, like sheep without a shepherd." We have heard these words so many times that perhaps they do not strike us powerfully. But they are powerful! A little like the many people whom you meet today on the streets of your own neighborhoods. . . . Then the horizon broadens, and we see that these towns and villages are not only Rome and Italy; they are the world . . . and those helpless crowds are the peoples of many nations who are suffering through even more difficult situations. . . .

Thus we understand that we are not here to take part in a pleasant retreat at the beginning of Lent, but rather to hear the voice of the Spirit speaking to the whole Church of our time, which is the time of mercy. I am sure of this. It is not only Lent; we are living in a time of mercy, and have been for thirty years or more, up to today.

1. IN THE CHURCH, EVERYTHING IS
THE TIME OF MERCY

This was an intuition of Bl. John Paul II. He "sensed" that this was the time of mercy. We think of the Beatification and Canonization of Sr. Faustina Kowalska; then he introduced the Feast of Divine Mercy. Little by little he advanced and went forward on this.

In his homily for the Canonization, which took place in 2000, John Paul II emphasized that the message of Jesus Christ to Sr. Faustina is located, in time, between the two World Wars and is intimately tied to the history of the twentieth century. And looking to the future he said: "What will the years ahead bring us? What will man's future on earth be like? We are not given to know. However, it is certain that in addition to new progress there will unfortunately be no lack of painful experiences. But the light of divine mercy, which the Lord in a way wished to return to the world through Sr. Faustina's charism, will illumine the way for the men and women of the third millennium" (Homily, Sunday, April 30, 2000). It is clear. Here it is explicit, in 2000, but it was something that had been maturing in his heart for some time. Through his prayer, he had this intuition.

Today we forget everything far too quickly, even the Magisterium of the Church! Part of this is unavoidable, but we cannot forget the great content, the great intuitions and gifts that have been left to the People of God. And Divine Mercy is one of these. It is a gift which he gave to us, but which comes from above. It is up to us, as ministers of the Church, to keep this message alive, above all through preaching and in our actions, in signs and in pastoral choices, such as the decision to restore priority to the Sacrament of Reconciliation and to the works of mercy. Reconciliation, making peace through the Sacrament, also with words, and with works of mercy.

2. WHAT DOES MERCY MEAN FOR PRIESTS?

It occurs to me that some of you have phoned, written a letter, then I spoke on the phone . . . "But Father, what have you got against priests?" Because they were saying that I bash priests! I do not wish to bash you here. . . .

Let us ask ourselves what mercy means for a priest, allow me to say for us priests. For us, for all of us! Priests are moved to compassion before the sheep, like Jesus, when he saw the people harassed and helpless, like sheep without a shepherd. Jesus has the "bowels" of God, Isaiah speaks about it very much: he is full of tenderness for the people, especially for those who are excluded, that is, for sinners, for the sick who no one takes care of. . . . Thus, in the image of the Good Shepherd, the priest is a man of mercy and compassion, close to his people and a servant to all. This is a pastoral criterion I would like to emphasize strongly: closeness. Closeness and service, but closeness, nearness! . . . Whoever is wounded in life, in whatever way, can find in him attention and a sympathetic ear. . . . The priest reveals a heart especially in administering the Sacrament of Reconciliation; he reveals it by his whole attitude, by the manner in which he welcomes, listens, counsels and absolves. . . . But this comes from how he experiences the Sacrament firsthand, from how he allows himself to be embraced by God the Father in Confession and remains in this embrace. . . . If one experiences this in one's own regard, in his own heart, he can also give it to others in his ministry. And I leave you with the question: How do I confess? Do I allow myself to be embraced? A great priest from Buenos Aires comes to mind, he is younger than I, he is around the age of seventy-two. . . . Once he came to see me. He is a great confessor: there are always people waiting in line for him there. . . . The majority of priests confess to him. . . . He is a great confessor. And once he came to see me: "But Father . . ."; "Tell me"; "I have a small scruple, because I know that I forgive too much!"; "Pray . . . if you forgive too much . . ." And we spoke about mercy. At a certain point he said to me: "You know, when I feel this scruple keenly, I go to the chapel, before the Tabernacle, and I say to Him: Excuse me, but it's Your fault, because it is you who has given me the bad example! And I go away at peace . . ." It is a beautiful prayer of mercy! If one experiences this in his own regard in Confession, in his own heart, he is able to give it to others.

The priest is called to learn this, to have a heart that is moved. Priests who are—allow me to say the word—"aseptic," those "from the laboratory," all clean and tidy, do not help the Church. Today we can think of the Church as a "field hospital." Excuse me but I repeat it, because this is how I see it, how I feel it is: a "field hospital." Wounds need to be treated, so many wounds! So many wounds! There are so many people who are wounded by material problems, by scandals, also in the Church . . . people wounded by the world's illusions. . . . We priests must be there, close to these people. Mercy first means treating the wounds. When someone is wounded, he needs this immediately, not tests such as the level of cholesterol and one's glycemic index. . . . But there's a wound, treat the wound, and then we can look at the results of the tests. Then specialized treatments can be done, but first we need to treat the open wounds. I think this is what is most important at this time. And there are also hidden wounds, because there are people who distance themselves in order to avoid showing their wounds closer. . . . The custom comes to mind, in the Mosaic Law, of the lepers in Jesus' time, who were always kept at a distance in order not to spread the contagion. . . . There are people who distance themselves through shame, through shame, so as not to let their wounds be seen. . . . And perhaps they distance themselves with some bitterness against the Church, but deep down inside there is a wound. . . . They want a caress! And you, dear brothers—I ask you—do you know the wounds of your parishioners? Do you perceive them? Are you close to them? It's the only question . . .

3. MERCY MEANS NEITHER GENEROSITY NOR RIGIDITY

Let us return to the Sacrament of Reconciliation. It often happens that we priests hear our faithful telling us they have encountered a very "strict" priest in the confessional, or very "generous," i.e., a *rigorist* or a *laxist*. And this is not good. It is normal that there be differences in the style of confessors, but these differences cannot regard the essential, that is, sound moral doctrine and mercy. Neither the laxist nor the rigorist bears witness to Jesus Christ, for neither the one nor the other takes care of the person he encounters. The rigorist washes his hands of them: in fact, he nails the person to the law, understood in a cold and rigid way; and the laxist also washes his hands of them: he is only apparently merciful, but in reality he does not take seriously the problems of that conscience, by minimizing the sin. True mercy *takes the person into one's care*, listens to him attentively, approaches the situation with respect and truth, and accompanies him on the journey of reconciliation. And this is demanding, yes, certainly. The truly merciful priest behaves like the Good Samaritan . . . but why does he do it? Because his heart is capable of having compassion, it is the heart of Christ!

We are well aware that *neither laxity nor rigorism foster holiness.*
Perhaps some rigorists seem holy, holy. . . . But think of Pelagius and then
let's talk. . . . Neither laxity nor rigorism sanctify the priest, and they do
not sanctify the faithful! However, mercy accompanies the journey of
holiness, it accompanies it and makes it grow. . . . Too much work for a
parish priest? It is true, too much work! And how do we accompany and
foster the journey of holiness? Through pastoral suffering, which is a form
of mercy. What does pastoral suffering mean? It means suffering for and
with the person. And this is not easy! To suffer like a father and mother
suffer for their children; I venture to say, also with anxious concern. . . .

To explain, I'll put to you some questions that help me when a priest
comes to me. They also help me when I am alone before the Lord!

Tell me: Do you weep? Or have we lost our tears? I remember that in
the old Missals, those of another age, there is a most beautiful prayer to
ask the gift of tears. The prayer began like this: "Lord, who commanded
Moses to strike the rock so that water might gush forth, strike the stone
of my heart so that tears . . .": the prayer went more or less like this. It
was very beautiful. But, how many of us weep before the suffering of a
child, before the breakup of a family, before so many people who do not
find the path? . . .The weeping of a priest. . . . Do you weep? Or in this
presbyterate have we lost all tears?

Do you weep for your people? Tell me, do you offer intercessory
prayer before the Tabernacle?

Do you struggle with the Lord for your people, as Abraham struggled?

"Suppose they were fewer? Suppose there were twenty-five? And
suppose they were twenty? . . . (cf. Gn 18:22-33). This courageous prayer
of intercession. . . . We speak of *parrhesia*, of apostolic courage, and we
think of pastoral plans, this is good, but the same *parrhesia* is also needed
in prayer. Do you struggle with the Lord? Do you argue with the Lord as
Moses did? When the Lord was annoyed, tired of his people, he said to
him: "Don't worry. . . . I will destroy everything, and I will make you the
head of another people." "No. No. If you destroy the people, destroy me
too." But, these were real men! Do we have enough guts to struggle with
God for our people?

Another question I ask: In the evening, how do you conclude your
day? With the Lord or in front of the television? How is your relationship with those who help you to be more merciful? That is, how is your

relationship with the children, with the elderly, with the sick? Do you know how to reassure them, or are you embarrassed to caress an elderly person?

Do not be ashamed of the flesh of your brother (cf. *Reflexiones en esperanza*, Ch. 1). In the end, we will be judged on our ability to draw close to "all flesh"—this is Isaiah. Do not be ashamed of the flesh of your brother. "Making ourselves close": closeness, nearness, being close to the flesh of one's brother. The priest and the Levite who had passed by before the Good Samaritan did not know how to draw close to the person who had been beaten by bandits. Their hearts were closed. Perhaps the priest had looked at his watch and said: "I have to go to Mass, I cannot be late for Mass," and he left. Excuses! How often we justify ourselves, to get around the problem, the person. The other, the Levite, or the doctor of the law, the lawyer, said: "No, I cannot because if I do this tomorrow I will have to go and testify, I will lose time . . ." Excuses! . . . Their hearts were closed. But a closed heart always justifies itself for what it has not done. Instead, the Samaritan opens his heart, he allows his heart to be moved, and this interior movement translates into practical action, in a concrete and effective intervention to help the person.

At the end of time, only those who have not been ashamed of the flesh of their brother who is injured and excluded will be permitted to contemplate the glorified flesh of Christ.

I admit, sometimes it does me good to read the list on which I will be judged, it benefits me: it is contained in Matthew 25.

These are the things that came to my mind to share with you. It is a bit rough and ready as things came to mind. . . . [Cardinal Vallini: "A good examination of conscience."] It will do us good. [applause]

In Buenos Aires—I am speaking of another priest—there was a well-known confessor: he was a Sacramentine. Almost all of the priests confessed to him. On one of the two occasions he came, John Paul II had requested a confessor at the Nunciature, and he went. He was old, very old. . . . He had served as Provincial in his Order, as a professor . . . but always as a confessor, always. And a long line was always awaiting him in the Church of the Most Blessed Sacrament. At the time, I was Vicar General and was living in the Curia, and every morning, early, I would go down to the fax to see if anything was there. And on Easter morning I read a fax from the community superior: "Yesterday, a half hour before the Easter Vigil, Fr. Aristi died at the age of ninety-four—or ninety-six? The funeral will be on such and such a day . . ." And on Easter morning I was to go to lunch with the priests at the retirement home—I usually did on Easter—and then—I said to myself—after lunch I will go to the Church. It was a large church, very large, with a beautiful crypt. I went down into the crypt and the coffin was there; only two old ladies were praying there, but not a single flower. I thought: but this man, who forgave the sins of all the clergy of Buenos Aires, including mine, not even a flower. . . . I went up and went to a florist—because in Buenos Aires there are flower shops at the crossroads, on the streets, where there are people—and I bought flowers, roses. . . . And I returned and began to decorate the coffin with flowers. . . . And I looked at the Rosary in his hands. . . . And immediately it came to mind—the thief that we all have inside of us, don't we?—And while I was arranging the flowers I took the cross off the Rosary, and with a little effort I detached it. At that moment I looked at him and said: "Give me half of your mercy." I felt something powerful that gave me the courage to do this and to say this prayer! And then I put the cross here, in my pocket. But the Pope's shirts don't have pockets, but I always carry it here in a little cloth bag, and that cross has been with me from that moment until today. And when a uncharitable thought against someone comes to mind, my hand always touches it here, always. And I feel the grace! I feel its benefit. What good the example of a merciful priest does, of a priest who draws close to wounds. . . .

If you think about it, surely you have known many, many of them, because Italian priests are good! They are good. I believe that if Italy is still so strong, it is not because of us who are Bishops, rather it is because of the parish priests, the priests! It is true, this is true! It is not a little incense to comfort you, I truly believe it to be so.

Mercy. Think of the many priests who are in heaven and ask of them this grace! May they grant you the mercy they had with their faithful. This does good.

Thank you for having listened and for having come here.

The Joy of Being Priests and the Beauty of Fraternity

Speech Prepared by the Holy Father and Given During the Meeting with Diocesan Priests of the Cathedral (Cassano all'Jonio)

June 21, 2014

Dear Priests,

I thank you for your welcome! I have looked forward to this meeting with you who carry the daily weight of parish work.

I would like first of all to share with you *the joy of being priests*. The ever new surprise of having been called, rather, of having been called by the Lord Jesus. Called to follow Him, to be with Him, to share His word with others, His forgiveness. . . . There's nothing finer for a man than this, isn't it true? When we priests are before the tabernacle, and we pause there for a moment, in silence, we then feel Jesus' gaze upon us once more, this gaze renews us, reinvigorates us. . . .

Of course, at times it's not easy to be before the Lord; it's not easy because we have so many things to do, so many people. . . . But at times it's not easy because we feel a certain discomfort, Jesus' gaze is a little unsettling, even causes us distress. . . . But this is good for us! In the silence of prayer Jesus shows us whether we are working well, like good workmen, or whether we may have become more like "employees"; whether we are open and generous "channels" through which his love, his grace flow in abundance, or whether we focus on ourselves, and thus instead of being "channels" we become "screens" which do not promote the encounter with the Lord, with the light and the power of the Gospel.

And the second thing I should like to share with you is *the beauty of fraternity*: of being priests together, of following the Lord not alone, not one by one, but together, and also in the great variety of gifts and personalities. Indeed, this is precisely what enriches the presbyterate, this variety of background, of age, of talents. . . . And all lived in communion, in fraternity.

This is neither easy nor immediate and we cannot take it for granted. First of all because even we priests are immersed in the subjectivistic overlay of today's culture, this culture which glorifies the "I" to the point of idolizing it. And then due to a certain pastoral individualism which is, unfortunately, widespread in our dioceses. This is why we have to react by choosing fraternity. I am intentionally speaking about "choice." This cannot just be left to chance, to fortuitous circumstances. . . . No, it's a choice, which corresponds to the reality that constitutes us, to the gift that we have received but that must always be heard and cultivated: communion in Christ in the presbytery, around the Bishop. This communion demands to be lived by seeking concrete forms adapted to the times and to the reality of the region, but always in an apostolic perspective, with a missionary lifestyle, with fraternity and simplicity of life. When Jesus says: "By this all men will know that you are my disciples, if you have love for one another" (Jn 13:35), He is certainly saying it to everyone, but first of all to the Twelve, to those He called to follow Him more closely.

The joy of being priests and the beauty of fraternity. These are the two things I felt were the most important when thinking about you. One last thing I'll just touch on: I encourage you in your work with families and for the family. This is work that the Lord asks us to do in a special way in these times, which are difficult times both for *the family* as an institution, and for *families* due to the crisis. But just when times are tough, God lets us feel His closeness, His grace, the prophetic strength of His Word. And we are called to be witnesses, mediators of this closeness to families and of this prophetic strength for the family.

Dear brothers, I thank you. Let us go forth, invigorated by the common love for the Lord and for the Holy Mother Church. May Our Lady protect you and go with you. Let us remain united in prayer. Thank you!

Sharing in the Pain of Jesus to the Very End

Meeting with Priests, Religious, and Seminarians

Church of Gethsemane at the Foot of the Mount of Olives, Jerusalem, May 26, 2014

"He came out and went . . . to the Mount of Olives; and the disciples followed him" (Lk 22:39).

At the hour which God had appointed to save humanity from its enslavement to sin, Jesus came here, to Gethsemane, to the foot of the Mount of Olives. We now find ourselves in this holy place, a place sanctified by the prayer of Jesus, by his agony, by his sweating of blood, and above all by his "yes" to the loving will of the Father. We dread in some sense to approach what Jesus went through at that hour; we tread softly as we enter that inner space where the destiny of the world was decided.

In that hour, Jesus felt the need to pray and to have with him his disciples, his friends, those who had followed him and shared most closely in his mission. But here, at Gethsemane, following him became difficult and uncertain; they were overcome by doubt, weariness and fright. As the events of Jesus' passion rapidly unfolded, the disciples would adopt different attitudes before the Master: attitudes of closeness, distance, hesitation.

Here, in this place, each of us—bishops, priests, consecrated persons, and seminarians—might do well to ask: Who am I, before the sufferings of my Lord?

Am I among those who, when Jesus asks them to keep watch with him, fall asleep instead, and rather than praying, seek to escape, refusing to face reality?

Or do I see myself in those who fled out of fear, who abandoned the Master at the most tragic hour in his earthly life?

Is there perhaps duplicity in me, like that of the one who sold our Lord for thirty pieces of silver, who was once called Jesus' "friend," and yet ended up by betraying him?

Do I see myself in those who drew back and denied him, like Peter? Shortly before, he had promised Jesus that he would follow him even unto death (cf. Lk 22:33); but then, put to the test and assailed by fear, he swore he did not know him.

Am I like those who began planning to go about their lives without him, like the two disciples on the road to Emmaus, foolish and slow of heart to believe the words of the prophets (cf. Lk 24:25)?

Or, thanks be to God, do I find myself among those who remained faithful to the end, like the Virgin Mary and the Apostle John? On Golgotha, when everything seemed bleak and all hope seemed pointless, only love proved stronger than death. The love of the Mother and the beloved disciple made them stay at the foot of the Cross, sharing in the pain of Jesus, to the very end.

Do I recognize myself in those who imitated their Master to the point of martyrdom, testifying that he was everything to them, the incomparable strength sustaining their mission and the ultimate horizon of their lives?

Jesus' friendship with us, his faithfulness and his mercy, are a priceless gift which encourages us to follow him trustingly, notwithstanding our failures, our mistakes, also our betrayals.

But the Lord's goodness does not dispense us from the need for vigilance before the Tempter, before sin, before the evil and the betrayal which can enter even into the religious and priestly life. We are all exposed to sin, to evil, to betrayal. We are fully conscious of the disproportion between the grandeur of God's call and of our own littleness, between the sublimity of the mission and the reality of our human weakness. Yet the Lord in his great goodness and his infinite mercy always takes us by the hand lest we drown in the sea of our fears and anxieties. He is ever at our side, he never abandons us. And so, let us not be overwhelmed by fear or disheartened, but with courage and confidence let us press forward in our journey and in our mission.

You, dear brothers and sisters, are called to follow the Lord with joy in this holy land! It is a gift and also a responsibility. Your presence here is extremely important; the whole Church is grateful to you and she sustains you by her prayers. From this holy place, I wish to extend my heartfelt greetings to all Christians in Jerusalem: I would like to assure them that I remember them affectionately and that I pray for them, being well aware of the difficulties they experience in this city. I urge them to be courageous witnesses of the passion of the Lord but also of his resurrection, with joy and hope.

Let us imitate the Virgin Mary and St. John, and stand by all those crosses where Jesus continues to be crucified. This is how the Lord calls us to follow him: this is the path, there is no other!

"Whoever serves me must follow me, and where I am, there will my servant be also" (Jn 12:26).

Having the Ability to Open Oneself to Diocesan Life

Meeting with the Priests of the Diocese of Caserta

Palatine Chapel in the Royal Palace of Caserta, July 26, 2014

Msgr. D'Alise, Bishop of Caserta:

Your Holiness, I did not prepare a written text because I immediately realized that you want a deep and intimate relationship with the priests. So I say to you "welcome." This is our Church, the priests, and then we will see the rest of the Church, as we celebrate the Eucharist. For me, this moment is important, because I have been here for only two months, and to begin this episcopate with Your presence and Your blessing is for me a grace within the grace. And now we await your words. Knowing that you would like to converse with the priests, they have also prepared some questions for you.

Holy Father:

I prepared a speech but I will give it to the Bishop. Thank you very much for the welcome. Thank you. I am happy and I feel a little guilty for having caused so many problems on the day of the patron's feast. But I did not know. And when I called the Bishop to tell him that I wanted to come and make a private visit here to a friend, Pastor Traettino, he said to me: "Ah, right on the patron saint's day!" And I immediately thought: "In the newspapers the next day it will read: 'on the patron feast of Caserta, Pope visits Protestants!'" Nice headline, eh? And, in this way, we organized the visit, a little rushed, but the Bishop helped me a lot as did the people at the Secretariat of State. I told the Substitute when I called him: "Please cut the cord from around my neck." He did so nicely. Thank you for the questions you will ask. We can begin; ask the questions and I will see if we can combine two or three, otherwise, I will respond to each one.

Your Holiness, thank you. I am the vicar general of Caserta, Fr. Pasquariello. A huge thank you for your visit to Caserta. I would like to ask a question: the good that you are bringing into the Catholic Church, with your daily homilies, official documents, especially Evangelii Gaudium, *focus mainly on spiritual, intimate, personal conversion. It is a reform that engages, in my humble opinion, only the sphere of theology, biblical exegesis and philosophy. Alongside this personal conversion, which is essential for eternal salvation, I would see as useful some intervention, on the part of Your Holiness, which could get the People of God more involved, precisely as people. Let me explain. Our diocese, for 900 years, has had absurd boundaries: some municipalities are divided in half between the dioceses of Capua and Acerra. In fact, the station of the city of Caserta, less than one kilometer away from City Hall, belongs to Capua. For this reason, Most Blessed Father, I ask for a decisive action so that our communities no longer have to suffer unnecessary travel and so that the pastoral unity of our faithful is no longer sacrificed. It is clear, Your Holiness, that in* Evangelii Gaudium, *no. 10, you say that these things belong to the episcopate. But I remember that as a young priest— forty-seven years ago—we went with Msgr. Roberti—he had come from the Secretariat of State—and we had brought a few problems even there; they said, after having explained things: "Come to an agreement with the bishops and we will sign." And this is a beautiful thing. But when will the bishops come to an agreement?*

Some Church historians say that in some of the first Councils, the Bishops would get to the point of punches but then they would come to an agreement. And this is a bad sign. It is bad when Bishops speak against each other or are roped in. I don't mean unity of thought or unity of spirituality, because this is good, I say roped in in the negative sense. This is bad because it breaks the unity of the Church. This is not of God. And we Bishops need to give the example of unity that Jesus asks of the Father for the Church. But we cannot go about speaking against one another: "And he does it this way and he does it that way . . ." Go on, say it to the person's face! Our ancestors at the first Councils got to the point of punches and I prefer that they yell a few strong words to each other and then embrace, rather than speak against each other in hiding. This, as a general principle, namely: in the unity of the Church, unity among

Bishops is important. You underlined the path that the Lord wanted for his Church. And this unity between Bishops is that which favors coming to an agreement on this or that issue. In one country—not in Italy, another place—there is a diocese whose boundaries have been reconfigured but motivated by the location of the cathedral's treasure, they have been discussed in court for more than forty years. For money: this is not understandable! This is where the devil rejoices! It is he who profits. It is nice then that you say the Bishops must always be in agreement: but agreement in unity, not in uniformity. Each person has his charism; each person has his way of thinking, of seeing things: this variety is sometimes the fruit of mistakes, but many times it is the fruit of the Spirit. The Holy Spirit wanted this variety of charisms to exists in the Church. The same Spirit that creates diversity then succeeds to create unity; unity in the diversity of each one, without each one losing his own personality. But, I hope that what you said will move ahead. And then, we are all good, because we all have the water of Baptism, we have the Holy Spirit within, who helps us to move ahead.

I am Fr. Angelo Piscopo, parish priest of San Pietro Apostolo and San Pietro in Cattedra. My question is this: Your Holiness, in the Apostolic Exhortation Evangelii Gaudium, you invited us to encourage and to reinforce popular piety, as the precious treasure of the Catholic Church. At the same time, however, you showed the risk—unfortunately, ever more real—of the diffusion of an individualistic and sentimental Christianity, more attentive to traditional forms and to revelation, deprived of the fundamental aspects of the faith and irrelevant to social life. What suggestion can you give us for a ministry that, without devaluing popular piety, can relaunch the primacy of the Gospel? Thank you, Your Holiness.

We hear that this is a time where religiosity has declined, but I do not believe so. Because there are these currents, these schools of intimist religiosity, like the gnostics, who have an approach similar to pre-Christian prayer, pre-biblical prayer, gnostic prayer, and gnosticism entered into the Church in these groups of intimist piety: I call this "intimism." "Intimism" is not good. It is something for me; I am calm; I feel full of God. It is a bit—it is not the same—but it is similar to *New Age*. There is religiosity, yes, but a pagan religiosity, even heretical. We must not be afraid to pronounce this word because gnosticism is a heresy. It was the Church's first heresy. When I speak of religiosity, I speak of that treasure of piety, with many values, which the great Paul VI describes in *Evangelii Nuntiandi*. Think of this: the *Document of Aparecida*, which was the document of the Fifth Conference of the Latin American Episcopate, in order to summarize at the end of the document, in the penultimate paragraph—because the last two were credits and prayers—had to go back forty years and extract a piece from *Evangelii Nuntiandi*, which is the post-Conciliar pastoral document that has yet to be surpassed. It is of great currency. In that document, Paul VI describes popular piety, affirming that sometimes it needs to be evangelized. Yes, because like every piety, it risks going a little this way and a little that way or not having an expression of strong faith. But the piety that people have, the piety that enters into the heart through Baptism has enormous strength, to the point that the People of God who have this piety, on the whole, can do no wrong. It is infallible *in credendo*: as said in *Lumen Gentium*, number 12. True popular piety is born from that *sensus fidei* of which this conciliar document speaks and it guides in the devotion to the Saints, to Our Lady, even with folk expressions in the good sense of the word. For this, popular piety is fundamentally enculturated. It cannot be a popular piety created in a laboratory, ascetic, but always born from our lives. Small mistakes can be made—therefore we must be vigilant—however, popular religiosity is a tool of evangelization. Let us think of today's young people. Young people—at least the experience I had in the other diocese—young people, youth movements in Buenos Aires did not work. Why? One would say to them: let's organize a meeting to talk . . . and in the end the young people got bored. But when pastors found a way to involve young people in small missions, to do a mission during vacation time, to give catechesis to people who needed it, in the small villages where there are no priests, then they adhered. Young people truly want this missionary role and they learn from it to live a form of piety that we can even say is popular piety: the missionary apostolate of young people has something of popular piety in it. Popular piety is active, it is a sense of faith—says Paul VI—deep, which only the simple and the humble are able to have. And this is great! In Shrines, for example, we see miracles! Every July 27, I would go to the St. Pantaleon Shrine in Buenos

Aires and I would listen to confessions in the morning. I would return renewed from that experience, I would return shamed by the holiness I would find in simple people, sinners but holy, because they would tell of their sins and recount how they lived, the problem of their son or their daughter or of this or the other, and how they would visit the sick. You could feel the Gospel. In Shrines, you find these things. The confessionals of Shrines are a place of renewal for us priests and Bishops; they are a course in spiritual renewal because of this contact with popular piety. And the faithful, when they come to confess, they tell you their miseries, but you see behind those miseries the grace of God that guides them to this moment. This contact with the People of God who pray, a pilgrim people, who manifest their faith in this form of piety, helps us a lot in our priestly life.

Allow me to call you father Francis because fatherhood inevitably implies holiness when it is authentic. As a pupil of the Jesuit fathers, to whom I owe my cultural and priestly formation, I will first share my thoughts and then ask a question that I will put to you in a special way. The identikit of the priest of the third millennium: human and spiritual balance; missionary consciousness; openness to dialogue with other faiths, religious and non. Why this? You certainly have brought about a Copernican revolution in terms of language, lifestyle, behavior and witness on the most considerable issues at a global level, even with atheists and with those who are far from the Catholic Christian Church. The question I ask you: How is it possible in this society, with a Church that hopes for growth and development, in this society with an evolution that is dynamic and conflictual and very often distant from the values of the Gospel of Christ, that we are a Church that is very often late? Your linguistic, semantic, cultural revolution, your evangelical witness is stirring an existential crisis for us priests. What imaginative and creative ways do you suggest for us to use in order to overcome or at least to alleviate this crisis that we perceive? Thank you.

So. How is it possible, with the Church growing and developing, to move forward? You said a few things: balance, openness to dialogue. . . . But, how can one go forward? You said a word that I really like. It is a divine word. If it is human it is because it is a gift of God: *creativity*. It is

the commandment God gave to Adam, "Go and multiply. Be *creative*."
It is also the commandment that Jesus gave to his disciples, through
the Holy Spirit, for example, the creativity of the early Church in her
relationship with Judaism: Paul was creative; Peter, that day when he
went to Cornelius, was afraid of them, because he was doing something
new, something creative. But he went there. Creativity is the word. And
how can you find this creativity? First of all—and this is the condition
if we want to be creative *in the* Spirit, that is to say in the Spirit of the
Lord Jesus—there is no other way than prayer. A Bishop who does not
pray, a priest who does not pray has closed the door, has closed the path
of creativity. It is precisely in prayer, when the Spirit makes you feel
something, the devil comes and makes you feel another; but prayer is
the condition for moving forward. Even if prayer can often seem boring.
Prayer is so important. Not only the prayer of the Divine Office, but the
liturgy of the Mass, quiet, celebrated well with devotion, personal prayer
with the Lord.

If we do not pray, perhaps we will be good pastoral and spiritual
entrepreneurs, but the Church without prayer becomes an NGO, she
does not have that *unctio Sancti Spiritu*. Prayer is the first step, because
one must open oneself to the Lord to be able to be open to others. It is
the Lord that says, "Go here, go there, do this . . . ," you will be inspired
by the creativity that was very costly for many saints. Think of Blessed
Antonio Rosmini, who wrote *The Five Wounds of the Church*, he was
really a creative critic because he prayed. He wrote that which the Spirit
made him feel. For this, he entered a spiritual prison, that is, in his home:
he could not speak, he could not teach, he could not write, his books
were placed on the Index. Today, he is Blessed! Many times creativity
brings you to the cross. But when it comes from prayer, it bears fruit.
Not creativity that is a little *sans façon* and revolutionary, because today
it is fashionable to be a revolutionary; no, this is not of the Spirit. But
when creativity comes from the Spirit and is born in prayer it can bring
you problems. Creativity that comes from prayer has an anthropological
dimension of transcendence, because through prayer you open yourself to
transcendence, to God.

But there is also another transcendence: opening oneself up to
others, to one's neighbor. We must not be a Church closed in on herself,
which watches her navel, a self-referential Church, who looks at herself

and is unable to transcend. Twofold transcendence is important: toward God and toward one's neighbor. Coming out of oneself is not an adventure; it is a journey, it is the path that God has indicated to men, to the people from the first moment when he said to Abraham, "Go from your country." He had to go out of himself. And when I come out of myself, I meet God and I meet others. How do you meet others? From a distance or up close? You must meet them up close, closeness. Creativity, transcendence and closeness. Closeness is a key word: be near. Do not be afraid of anything. Be close. The man of God is not afraid. Paul himself, when he saw the many idols in Athens, was not afraid. He said to the people: "You are religious, many idols . . . but, I will speak to you about another." He did not get scared and he got close to them. He also cited their poets: "As your poets say . . ." It's about closeness to a culture, closeness to the people, to their way of thinking, their sorrows, their resentments. Many times this closeness is just a penance, because we need to listen to boring things, to offensive things.

Two years ago, a priest who went to Argentina as a missionary—he was from the Diocese of Buenos Aires and went to a diocese in the south, to an area where for years they had no priest, and the evangelicals had arrived—told me that he went to a woman who had been the teacher of the people and then the principle of the village school. This lady sat him down and began insulting him, not with bad words, but insulting him forcefully: "You abandoned us, you left us alone, and I, who need the Word of God, had to go to Protestant worship and I became a Protestant." This young priest, who is meek, who is one who prays, when the woman finished her discourse, said: "Madam, just one word: forgiveness. Forgive us, forgive us. We abandoned the flock." And the woman's tone changed. However, she remained Protestant and the priest did not go into the subject of which was the true religion. In that moment, this could not be done. In the end, the lady began to smile and said: "Father, would you like some coffee?"—"Yes, let's have a coffee." And when the priest was about to leave, she said: "Stop, Father. Come." And she led him into the bedroom, she opened the closet and there was the image of Our Lady: "You must know that I never abandoned her. I hid her because of the pastor, but she's in the home." It is a story that teaches how proximity, meekness brought about this woman's reconciliation with the Church, because she felt abandoned by the Church.

And I asked a question that you must never ask: "And then, how did things turn out? How did it end?" But the priest corrected me: "Oh, no, I did not ask anything: she continues to go to Protestant worship, but you can see that she is a woman who prays. The Lord Jesus provides." And he did not go beyond that, and he did not urge her to return to the Catholic Church. It is that prudent closeness, which knows just how far one can reach. But, closeness also means dialogue; you must read in *Ecclesiam Suam*, the doctrine on dialogue, later repeated by other Popes. Dialogue is so important, but to dialogue two things are necessary: one's identity as a starting point and empathy toward others. If I am not sure of my identity and I go to speak, I end up bartering my faith. You cannot dialogue without starting from your own identity, and empathy, which is *a priori* not condemning. Every man, every woman has something of their own to give us; every man, every woman has their own story, their own situation and we have to listen to it. Then the prudence of the Holy Spirit will tell us how to respond. Start from your own identity in order to dialogue, but a dialogue is not doing apologetics, although sometimes you must do so, when we are asked questions that require an explanation. Dialogue is a human thing. It is hearts and souls that dialogue, and this is so important! Do not be afraid to dialogue with anyone. It was said of a saint, joking somewhat—I do not remember, I think it was St. Philip Neri, but I'm not sure—that he was able to dialogue even with the devil. Why? Because he had that freedom to listen to all people, but starting from his own identity. He was so sure, but being sure of one's identity does not mean proselytizing. Proselytism is a trap, which even Jesus condemns a little, *en passant*, when he speaks to the Pharisees and the Sadducees: "You who go around the world to find a proselyte and then you remember that . . ." But, it's a trap. And Pope Benedict has a beautiful expression. He said it in Aparecida but I believe he repeated it elsewhere: "The Church grows not by proselytism, but by attraction." And what's the attraction? It is this human empathy, which is then guided by the Holy Spirit. Therefore, what will be the profile of the priest of this century, which is so secularized? A man of creativity, who follows God's commandment—"to create things"; a man of transcendence, both with God in prayer and with others always; a man who is approachable and who is close to the people. To distance people is not priestly and people are tired of this attitude, and yet they still come to

48

us. But he who welcomes the people and is close to them and dialogues with them does so because he feels certain of his identity, which leads him to have a heart open to empathy. This is what comes to me in response to your question.

Dear Father, my question is about the place where we live: the diocese, with our bishops, our relationships with our brothers and sisters. And I ask you: This historic time in which we are living has expectations of us as priests, that is of a clear, open, and joyful witness—as you are inviting us to be—in the newness of the Holy Spirit. I ask you: What would really be, in your opinion, the specific foundation of the diocesan priest's spirituality? I think I read somewhere that you say: "The priest is not a contemplative." But it was not like that before. So, if you could give us an icon that we can refer to for the rebirth, the communal growth of our diocese. And above all, I'm interested in how we can be faithful, today, to man, not so much to God.

Here, you said "the newness of the Holy Spirit." It's true. But God is a God of surprises. He always surprises us, always, always. We read the Gospel and we find one surprise after another. Jesus surprises us because he arrives before us: He waits for us first, he loves us first, when we seek Him, he is already looking for us. As the prophet Isaiah or Jeremiah says, I do not remember well: God is like the flower of the almond tree, the first to blossom in spring. He is first, always first, always waiting for us. And this is the surprise. So many times we seek God here and He waits for us there. And then we come to the spirituality of the diocesan clergy. A contemplative priest, but not like one who is in a Carthusian monastery, I do not mean this contemplativeness. The priest must have contemplativeness, an ability to contemplate both God and people. He is a man who looks, who fills his eyes and his heart with this contemplation: with the Gospel before God, and with human problems before men. In this sense, he must be a contemplative. One should not get confused: the monk is something else. But where is the focal point of the spirituality of the diocesan priest? I would say it is in diocesan life. It is having the ability to open oneself to diocesan life. The spirituality of a religious person, for example, is the ability to open up to God and to others in the community: be it the smallest or the largest congregation.

Instead, the spirituality of the diocesan priest is to be open to diocesan life. And you religious who work in the parish need to do both things, which is why the dicastery for Bishops and the dicastery for consecrated life are working on a new version of *Mutuae Relationes*, because the religious has the two affiliations. Let us return to "diocesan life": What does it mean? It means having a relationship with the Bishop and a relationship with the other priests. The relationship with the Bishop is important, it is necessary. A diocesan priest cannot be separated from the Bishop. "But the Bishop does not care for me, the Bishop here, the Bishop there . . .": The Bishop may perhaps be a man with a bad temper, but he's your Bishop. And you have to find, even in that non-positive attitude, a way to maintain a relationship with him. This, however, is the exception. I am a diocesan priest because I have a relationship with the Bishop, a necessary relationship. It is really significant when, during the rite of ordination, one makes the vow of obedience to the Bishop. "I pledge obedience to you and your successors." Diocesan life means a relationship with the Bishop, which must be realized and must grow continuously. In the majority of cases it is not a catastrophic problem, but a normal reality. Secondly, the diocesan life involves a relationship with the other priests, with all the presbytery. There is no spirituality of the diocesan priest without these two relationships: with the Bishop and with the presbytery. And they are needed. "I, yes, get along well with the Bishop, but I do not attend the clergy meetings because they make small talk." With this attitude, you are missing out on something: you do not have that true spirituality of the diocesan priest. That's it: it is simple, but at the same time it is not easy. It is not easy because reaching an agreement with the Bishop is not always easy, because one thinks in one way the other thinks in another way. You can discuss and discuss! And can it be done in a loud voice? It can! How many times does a son argue with his father and, in the end, they always remain father and son.

However, when in these two relationships, both with the Bishop and with the presbytery, diplomacy enters, the Spirit of the Lord is not there, because the spirit of freedom is lacking. We must have the courage to say, "I do not think of it that way; I think of it differently," and also the humility to accept a correction. It's very important. And what is the greatest enemy of these two relationships? Gossip. Many times I think—because I too have this urge to gossip, we have it inside us, the devil knows that this seed bears fruit and he sows it well—I think it is a consequence of a celibate life lived as sterility, not as fruitfulness. A lonely man ends up embittered, he is not fruitful and gossips about others. This is not good, this is precisely what prevents an evangelical, spiritual and fruitful relationship with the Bishop and the presbytery. Gossip is the strongest enemy of diocesan life, that is, of spirituality. But you are a man. Therefore, if you have something against the Bishop, go and tell him. But then there will be consequences. You will carry the cross, but be a man! If you are a mature man and you see something in your brother priest that you do not like or that you believe to be wrong, go and tell him to his face. Or if you see that he does not tolerate being corrected, go tell the Bishop or that priest's closest friend, so that he may help him correct himself. But do not tell others, because that's getting each other dirty. And the devil is happy with that "banquet" because that way he attacks the very center of the spirituality of the diocesan clergy. For me, gossip does so much damage. And I am not some post-Conciliar novelty. . . . St. Paul already had to deal with this. Remember the phrase: "I belong to Paul," or "I belong to Apollos. . . ." Gossip has been a reality since the beginning of the Church, because the devil does not want the Church to be a fertile mother, united, joyful. What instead is the sign that these two relationships, between priest and Bishop and between priest and the other priests, are going well? It is joy. Just as bitterness is the sign that there is no real diocesan spirituality, because a good relationship with the Bishop or the presbytery is lacking, joy is a sign that things are working. You can discuss, you can get angry, but there is joy above all, and it is important that it always remains in these two relationships which are essential to the spirituality of the diocesan priest.

I would like to return to another sign, the sign of bitterness. Once a priest told me, here in Rome: "But, I often see we are a Church of angry people, always angry with each other; we always have something to be angry about." This leads to sadness and bitterness: there is no joy. When we find a priest in a diocese who lives with anger and tension, we think: but this man has vinegar for breakfast. Then at lunch, pickled vegetables, and then in the evening some lemon juice. His life is not working because it is the image of a Church of angry people. Instead, joy is a sign that things are going well. You can get angry: it is even healthy to get angry once. But the state of anger is not of the Lord and it leads to sadness and disunity. And in the end, you said "fidelity to God and man." It is the same as we said before. It is twofold faithfulness and twofold transcendence: to be faithful to God is to seek him, to open oneself to Him in prayer, remembering that He is the faithful one. He cannot deny Himself; he is always faithful. And then opening oneself to others; it is that empathy, that respect, that listening, and saying the right word with patience.

We must stop in order to love the faithful who are waiting. . . . But I thank you, truly, and I ask you to pray for me, because even I have the difficulties of every Bishop and I have to resume the path of conversion every day. Prayer for each other will do us good to keep moving forward. Thank you for your patience.

Pastors Courageous in the Face of Difficulty and Trial

Celebration of Vespers with Priests, Religious, Seminarians, and Various Lay Movements

Cathedral of Tirana (Albania), September 21, 2014

The Pope Spoke Extemporaneously

We, who have been called by the Lord to follow him closely, must find our consolation in him alone. Woe to us if we seek consolation elsewhere! Woe to priests and religious, sisters and novices, consecrated men and women, when they seek consolation far from the Lord! Today I don't want to be harsh and severe with you, but I want you to realize very clearly that if you look for consolation anywhere else, you will not be happy! Even more, you will be unable to comfort others, for your own heart is closed to the Lord's consolation. You will end up, as the great Elijah said to the people of Israel, "limping with both legs."

"Blessed be the God and Father of our Lord Jesus Christ, the Father of mercies and the God of all consolation, who consoles us in all our affliction, so that we may be able to console those who are in any affliction with the consolation with which we ourselves are consoled by God."

Prepared Address

Since the moment your country has been free from dictatorship, the ecclesial communities in Albania have begun again to journey onward and to organize themselves for pastoral work, looking to the future with hope. I am particularly grateful to those Pastors who paid a great price for their fidelity to Christ and for their decision to remain united to the Successor of Peter. They were courageous in the face of difficulty and trial! There are still priests and religious among us who have experienced prison and persecution, like the sister and brother who have told us their story. I embrace you warmly, and I praise God for your faithful witness that inspires the whole Church to continue to proclaim the Gospel with joy. . . .

Evangelization is more effective when it is carried out with oneness of spirit and with sincere teamwork among the various ecclesial communities as well as among missionaries and local clergy: this requires courage to seek out ways of working together and offering mutual help in the areas of catechesis and Catholic education, as well as integral human development and charity. In these settings, the contribution of the ecclesial movements that know how to work in communion with Pastors is highly valuable. That is precisely what I see before me: bishops, priests, religious and laity: a Church that desires to walk in fraternity and unity.

When love for Christ is placed above all else, even above our legitimate particular needs, then we are able to move outside of ourselves, of our personal or communal pettiness, and move toward Jesus who, in our brothers and sisters, comes to us. . . .

Considering the fact that the number of priests and religious is not yet sufficient, the Lord Jesus repeats to you today, "The harvest is plentiful, but the laborers are few; pray therefore the Lord of the harvest to send out laborers into his harvest" (Mt 9:37-38). We must not forget that this prayer begins with a gaze: the gaze of Jesus, who sees the great harvest. Do we also have this gaze? Do we know how to recognize the abundant fruits that the grace of God has caused to grow and the work that there is to be done in the field of the Lord? It is by gazing with faith on the field of God that prayer springs forth, namely, the daily and pressing invocation to the Lord for priestly and religious vocations. . . . The people, more than seeking experts, are looking for witnesses: humble witnesses of the mercy and tenderness of God; priests and religious conformed to Jesus, the Good Shepherd, who are capable of communicating the love of Christ to all people.

Jesus Must Be at the Center of Life

Meeting with Priests, Religious, and Permanent Deacons

Naples Cathedral, March 21, 2015

Extemporaneous Speech

I prepared a speech, but speeches are boring. I shall consign it to the Cardinal and then he will publish it in the bulletin. I prefer to respond to a few things. They are telling me to speak sitting down, this way I can rest a bit. A very elderly nun who is here, quickly came up to me to say: "Please give me the blessing in *articulo mortis*."—"But why, Sister?"— "Because I must go on mission, to open a convent . . ." This is the spirit of religious life. This nun made me think. She is elderly, but she says: "Yes, I'm in *articulo mortis*, but I must go to renew or to once again open a convent" and she departs. Thus I too obey now and I'm speaking sitting down.

This is one of the forms of testimony that you asked about: to be ever journeying. The journey in consecrated life is following the footsteps of Jesus; for priests and for consecrated life in general, it is following Jesus, and with the will to work for the Lord. Once—I refer to what the sister said—an elderly priest said to me: "There is no retirement for us and when we go home to rest we continue to work with prayers, with the small things we are able to do, but with the same enthusiasm of following Jesus." The testimony of walking on the paths of Jesus! For this, Jesus must be at the center of life. If at the center of life—I'm exaggerating . . . it happens in other places, but certainly not in Naples—it may happen that I am against the bishop or against the parish priest or against that other priest, my whole life is taken up in that struggle. But this is wasting one's life. Not having a family, not having children, not having marital love, which is so good and so beautiful, to end up quarreling with the bishop, with brother priests, with the faithful, with a "sour face," this is not a testimony. Testimony is Jesus, the center is Jesus. And when the center is Jesus these difficulties are still there, they are everywhere, but they are faced in a different way. In a convent perhaps

I do not like the superior, but if my center is the superior whom I don't like, my testimony is not good. Instead, if my center is Jesus, I pray for this superior whom I don't like, I tolerate her and do my best since other superiors know the situation. But no one can take away my joy: joy is following Jesus. I see seminarians here. I'll tell you something: if you do not have Jesus at the center, delay your Ordination. If you are not certain that Jesus is the center of your life, wait a while longer, so as to be sure. Because on the contrary, you will begin a journey without knowing where it will lead.

This is the first testimony: Seeing Jesus at the center. The center is not gossip nor the ambition to have this post or that one, nor money—I shall speak about money later—but the center must be Jesus. How can I be sure I am always following Jesus? His Mother leads us to Him. A priest, a man or woman religious who does not love Our Lady, who does not pray to Our Lady, I would also say who does not recite the Rosary . . . if they do not want the Mother, the Mother will not give them the Son.

The Cardinal gave me a book by St. Alphonsus Maria de' Liguori, perhaps *The Glories of Mary*. . . . In this book, I enjoy reading the stories about Our Lady that are after each of the chapters: in them we see how Our Lady always leads us to Jesus. She is Mother, the center of Our Lady's being is being Mother, bearing Jesus. Fr. Rupnik who makes such beautiful and artistic paintings and mosaics, gave me an icon of Our Lady with Jesus in front. Jesus and Our Lady's hands are placed in such a way that Jesus is descending and holding onto the Madonna's cape with his hand so as not to fall. It is she who allowed Jesus come down to us; it is she who gives us Jesus. Bear witness to Jesus. And the Mother is a beautiful aid in following Jesus: it is she who gives us Jesus. This is one of the forms of testimony.

Another form of testimony is the spirit of poverty; even for priests who do not take the vow of poverty, but should have the spirit of poverty. When profiteering enters the Church, whether in priests or men and women religious, it is awful. I recall a great woman religious, a good woman, a great treasurer who was good at her work. She was observant but her heart was attached to money and she unconsciously chose people according to the money they had. "I like this one more, he has lots of money." She was the treasurer of an important college and constructed many great buildings, a great woman, but you could see this limitation of hers and this woman's ultimate humiliation was public. She was seventy years old, more or less, she was in a teachers' lounge, during a school break, having a coffee, when she had a fainting spell and fell. They slapped her to bring her round, but she didn't recover. And a teacher said this: "Put some 'pesos' in front of her and let's see if she responds." The poor woman was already dead, but this was the last word that was said about her when it wasn't yet known whether or not she would die. It was an awful testimony.

Consecrated people—be they priests, nuns or religious—must never be businesspeople. The spirit of poverty, however, is not the spirit of misery. A priest, who has not taken the vow of poverty, can have his savings, but in an honest and reasonable manner. But when he has avarice and goes into business . . . So many scandals in the Church and such a lack of freedom because of money: "I should take this person to task, but I cannot because he is a great benefactor." Since great benefactors live the life they want to I am not at liberty to do so, because I am attached to the money they give me. You see how important poverty is, the spirit of poverty, as the first of the Beatitudes says: "Blessed are the poor in spirit." As I said, a priest may keep his savings, but his heart must not be there, and the savings must be modest. When it is a question of money, people are appraised differently; this is why I ask everyone to examine their conscience: how is my life of poverty going, also what I receive from small things? This is the second form of testimony.

The third form of testimony—and I am speaking generally here, for religious and consecrated people and also for diocesan priests—is mercy. We have forgotten the works of mercy. I would like to—I shall not, but I would like to—ask you to recite the corporal works of mercy, and the spiritual ones. How many of us have forgotten them! When you return home take up the Catechism and look up these works of mercy which are the works performed by elderly women and simple people in the neighborhoods, parishes, because following Jesus, walking after Jesus is simple. I shall cite an example that I always use. In the large cities, still Christian cities—I am thinking of my former diocese, but I believe that the same happens in Rome, I don't know about Naples, but definitely in Rome—there are baptized children who don't know how to make the sign of the Cross. Where is the work of mercy of teaching in this case? "I shall teach you to make the sign of faith." It is only an example. We need to resume the works of mercy, both corporal and spiritual. If a neighbor is ill and I would like to go to visit him/her, but the time I have available coincides with the time for my soap opera, and between the soap opera and doing a work of mercy I choose the soap opera, this is not good.

Speaking of soap operas, I shall return to the spirit of poverty. In my previous diocese there was a college run by nuns, a good college, they worked hard, but in the building where they lived within the college there was a part that was the sisters' flat. The house where they lived was somewhat old and needed to be renovated, and they fixed it up well, too well, it was luxurious: they even put a television in every room. At soap opera time, you could not find one sister available in the college. . . . These are the things that lead to a worldly spirit, and this is where the other thing I would like to say comes in: the danger of worldliness. Living in a worldly manner. Living with the worldly spirit that Jesus didn't want! Think about the priestly prayer of Jesus when He prayed to the Father: "I do not pray that thou shouldst take them out of the world, but that thou shouldst keep them from the evil one" (Jn 17:15). Worldliness goes against testimony, while the spirit of prayer is a testimony that is seen: we see who are the consecrated men and women who pray, as well as those who pray formally but not with the heart. They are testimonies that people see. You spoke of the lack of vocations, but testimony is one of the things that attracts vocations. "I want to be like that priest, I want to be like that nun." The witness of life. A comfortable life, a worldly life does not help us. The Vicar for the Clergy has highlighted the problem, the fact—I call it a problem—of priestly fraternity. This also applies to consecrated life. Life, whether in the community of consecrated life or in the presbyterate, in the diocese, which is the real charism of diocesan priests, in the presbyterate around the bishop. Carrying on this "fraternity" is not easy in the convent, in consecrated life, or in the presbytery. The devil always tempts us with jealousy, envy, infighting, antipathy, sympathy, so many things that don't help us to live true fraternity, and thus we bear a testimony of division among ourselves.

To me, the sign that that there is no fraternity, whether in the presbyterate or in religious communities is when there is gossip. And allow me to use this expression: the terrorism of gossip, because one who gossips is a terrorist dropping a bomb, destroying from the outside—not even like a Kamikaze, but destroying others instead. Gossip destroys and is the sign that there is no fraternity. When someone meets a priest who has different views . . . because there are always differences, it's normal, it's Christian—these differences should be clarified with the courage to say it face to face. If I have something to say to the Bishop, I go to the Bishop and I can even say to him: "But, you are unpleasant," and the Bishop must have the courage not to seek revenge. This is brotherhood! Or when you have something against someone else and instead of going to him you go to another person. There are problems both in religious life and in presbyterial life, which must be addressed, but only between two people. If this cannot be done—because sometimes it can't be—tell it to someone who can act as an intermediary. But you must not speak against the other, because gossip is a form of terrorism that disrupts diocesan fraternity, priestly fraternity, religious communities.

Now, on to witness, to joy. The joy in my life is full, the joy of having chosen well, the joy that I see every day that the Lord is faithful to me. Joy is seeing that the Lord is always faithful to everyone. When I am not faithful to the Lord, I approach the Sacrament of Reconciliation. Consecrated men and women or priests who are bored, bitter of heart, who are sad, feel that something isn't right, need to go to a good spiritual advisor, a friend and say: "I don't know what's happening in my life." When there is no joy, something is wrong. The sense that the Archbishop spoke about today tells us that something is lacking. Without joy you do not attract the Lord and the Gospel.

These are the forms of testimony. I would like to conclude with three things. First: adoration. "Do you pray?"—"I pray, yes." I ask, I thank, I praise the Lord. But, do you adore the Lord? We have lost the meaning of the adoration of God: we must bring back the adoration of God. Second: you cannot love Jesus without loving his Bride. Love for the Church. We have met many priests who loved the Church and we saw that they loved her. Third, and this is important: apostolic zeal, that is, being a missionary. Love for the Church leads one to make her known, to go beyond oneself in order to go out and preach the Revelation of Jesus, but it also impels one to go beyond oneself to approach that other transcendence, namely adoration. In the context of being a missionary I think that the Church has to journey a little more, convert more, for the Church is not an NGO, but is the Bride of Christ who has the greatest treasure: Jesus. Her mission, her raison d'être is precisely this: to evangelize, in other words, to bring Jesus. Adoration, love for the Church and being a missionary. These are the three things that came to mind spontaneously.

After Venerating the Relic of St. Januarius's Blood

The Archbishop said that the blood has liquefied partially: so the Saint loves us partially. Everyone needs a little more conversion so that he loves us more. Thank you very much, and please, do not forget to pray for me.

Speech Prepared But Not Delivered

Dear Brothers and Sisters, good afternoon!

I thank you for your welcome in this symbolic place of faith and of the history of Naples: the Cathedral. Thank you, Your Eminence, for introducing our meeting; and thanks to the two brothers who asked questions on behalf of everyone.

I would like to begin from that expression that the Vicar for the Clergy said: "Being priests is beautiful." Yes, it is beautiful being priests, and being consecrated people too. I will first address the priests, and then the consecrated men and women.

I share with you *the ever new surprise of being called* by the Lord to follow Him, to be with Him, and to go toward the people bringing his word, his forgiveness. . . . It is truly a great thing that has happened to us, a grace of the Lord which is renewed every day. I imagine that in a busy reality such as Naples, with old and new challenges, you are thrown headlong to meet the needs of so many brothers and sisters, running the risk of becoming completely absorbed. We must always find time to remain in front of the Tabernacle, to pause there in silence, to feel Jesus' gaze upon us, which renews us and revives us. And should being in front of Jesus unsettle us somewhat, it is a good sign, it will do us good! It is precisely up to prayer to show us whether we are walking on the way of life or on that of falsehood, as the Psalm says (cf. 139[138]:24), if we work as good laborers or have become "employees," if we are open "channels," through which love and the grace of the Lord flow, or if we instead place ourselves at the center, eventually becoming "shields" that do not foster the encounter with the Lord.

Then there is *the beauty of fraternity*, of being priests together, of following the Lord not alone, not individually, but together, in the great variety of gifts and personalities, and all that is lived in community and fraternity. This too is not easy, nor immediate and expected, for even we priests live immersed in this subjectivistic culture of today, which exalts the "I" until idolatry. Then there is also a certain pastoral individualism, which carries the temptation of going forward alone, or with the small group of those who "think like I do." . . . Instead we know that everyone is called to experience communion with Christ in the presbytery, around the Bishop. Concrete forms which are appropriate for the times and the reality of the territory can—indeed must—always be sought, but this pastoral and missionary search should be done in an attitude of communion, with humility and fraternity.

Let us not forget the beauty of *walking with the people*. I know that for several years your diocesan community has undertaken an ongoing effort of rediscovering the faith, in contact with a city reality that wants to rise back up and needs everyone's cooperation. Therefore, I encourage you to go out to meet others, to open doors and reach out to families, the sick, young people, the elderly, there where they live, looking for them, being at their side, supporting them, in order to celebrate the liturgy of life with them. In particular, it will be beautiful *to accompany families in the challenge to generate and educate their children. Children* are a "diagnostic sign," to see the society's health. Children should not be spoiled, but should be loved! And we priests are called to accompany families in order that children may *be educated in Christian life*.

The second speech made reference to *consecrated life*, and mentioned lights and shadows. There is always a temptation to give more emphasis to the shadows, at the expense of light. This leads us, however, to fold in on ourselves, to continuously complain, to always blame others. And instead, especially during this Year of Consecrated Life, let us allow the beauty of our vocation to appear in us and in our communities, so it may be true that "where there are religious, there is joy." With this spirit I wrote the Letter to consecrated men and women, and I hope that it is helping you in your personal and communal journey. I would like to ask you: How is the "atmosphere" in your communities? Is there this gratitude, is there this joy of God who fills our heart? If this is there, then my hope has been realized that none of us be dour, discontented and dissatisfied, for "a gloomy disciple is a disciple of gloom" (*ibid.*, II, 1).

Dear consecrated brothers and sisters, I hope you may bear witness, with humility and simplicity, that consecrated life is a precious gift for the Church and for the world. A gift not to be withheld for oneself, but to share, bringing Christ to every corner of this city. May your daily gratitude to God find expression in the desire to draw hearts to Him, and to accompany them on the journey. Both in contemplative and apostolic life, may you feel strongly within you a love for the Church and contribute, through your specific charism, to her mission of proclaiming the Gospel and edifying the People of God in unity, in holiness and in love.

Dear brothers and sisters, I thank you. Let us go forth, animated by a common love for the Lord and for the holy Mother Church. I wholeheartedly bless you. And please, do not forget to pray for me.

All Pastoral Ministry Is Born of Love

Mass with Bishops, Priests, and Religious

Cathedral of the Immaculate Conception, Manila (Philippines), January 16, 2015

Said the Lord: "Do you love me? . . . Tend my sheep" (Jn 21:15-17). Jesus' words to Peter in today's Gospel are the first words I speak to you, dear brother bishops and priests, men and women religious, and young seminarians. These words remind us of something essential. All pastoral ministry is born of love. All pastoral ministry is born of love! All consecrated life is a sign of Christ's reconciling love. Like St. Therese, in the variety of our vocations, each of us is called, in some way, to be love in the heart of the Church. . . .

"The love of Christ impels us" (2 Cor 5:14). In today's first reading St. Paul tells us that the love we are called to proclaim is a reconciling love, flowing from the heart of the crucified Savior. We are called to be "ambassadors for Christ" (2 Cor 5:20). Ours is a ministry of reconciliation. We proclaim the Good News of God's infinite love, mercy and compassion. We proclaim the joy of the Gospel. For the Gospel is the promise of God's grace, which alone can bring wholeness and healing to our broken world. It can inspire the building of a truly just and redeemed social order.

To be an ambassador for Christ means above all to invite everyone to a renewed personal encounter with the Lord Jesus (*Evangelii Gaudium*, no. 3). Our personal encounter with Him. . . . But the Gospel is also a summons to conversion, to an examination of our consciences, as individuals and as a people. . . .

The Gospel calls individual Christians to live lives of honesty, integrity and concern for the common good. But it also calls Christian communities to create "circles of integrity," networks of solidarity which can expand to embrace and transform society by their prophetic witness.

The poor. The poor are at the center of the Gospel, are at heart of the Gospel, if we take away the poor from the Gospel we can't understand the whole message of Jesus Christ. As ambassadors for Christ, we, bishops, priests and religious, ought to be the first to welcome his reconciling grace into our hearts. St. Paul makes clear what this means. It means rejecting worldly perspectives and seeing all things anew in the light of Christ. It means being the first to examine our consciences, to acknowledge our failings and sins, and to embrace the path of constant conversion, every day conversion. How can we proclaim the newness and liberating power of the Cross to others, if we ourselves refuse to allow the word of God to shake our complacency, our fear of change, our petty compromises with the ways of this world, our "spiritual worldliness" (cf. *Evangelii Gaudium*, no. 93)?

For us priests and consecrated persons, conversion to the newness of the Gospel entails a daily encounter with the Lord in prayer. The saints teach us that this is the source of all apostolic zeal! For religious, living the newness of the Gospel also means finding ever anew in community life and community apostolates the incentive for an ever closer union with the Lord in perfect charity. For all of us, it means living lives that reflect the poverty of Christ, whose entire life was focused on doing the will of the Father and serving others. The great danger to this, of course, is a certain materialism which can creep into our lives and compromise the witness we offer. Only by becoming poor ourselves, by becoming poor ourselves, by stripping away our complacency, will we be able to identify with the least of our brothers and sisters. We will see things in a new light and thus respond with honesty and integrity to the challenge of proclaiming the radicalism of the Gospel in a society which has grown comfortable with social exclusion, polarization and scandalous inequality.

Here I would like to say a special word to the young priests, religious and seminarians among us. I ask you to share the joy and enthusiasm of your love for Christ and the Church with everyone, but especially with your peers. Be present to young people who may be confused and despondent, yet continue to see the Church as their friend on the journey and a source of hope. Be present to those who, living in the midst of a society burdened by poverty and corruption, are broken in spirit, tempted to give up, to leave school and to live on the streets. Proclaim the beauty and truth of the Christian message to a society which is tempted by confusing presentations of sexuality, marriage and the family. As you know, these realities are increasingly under attack from powerful forces which threaten to disfigure God's plan for creation and betray the very values which have inspired and shaped all that is best in your culture. . . .

Christ died for all so that, having died in him, we might live no longer for ourselves but for him (cf. 2 Cor 5:15). Dear brother bishops, priests and religious: I ask Mary, Mother of the Church, to obtain for all of you an outpouring of zeal, so that you may spend yourselves in selfless service to our brothers and sisters.

True Happiness Comes from Helping Others

Meeting with Priests, Religious, Seminarians, and Families of Survivors

Cathedral of the Transfiguration of Our Lord, Palo (Philippines), January 17, 2015

In a special way, I would like to thank the many priests and religious who responded with such overwhelming generosity to the desperate needs of the people. . . . By your presence and your charity, you bore witness to the beauty and truth of the Gospel. You made the Church present as a source of hope, healing and mercy. Together with so many of your neighbors, you also demonstrated the deep faith and the resilience of the Filipino people. The many stories of goodness and self-sacrifice which emerged from these dark days need to be remembered and passed down for future generations. . . .

Many of you showed heroic generosity in the aftermath of the typhoon. I hope that you will always realize that true happiness comes from helping others, giving ourselves to them in self-sacrifice, mercy and compassion. In this way you will be a powerful force for the renewal of society, not only in the work of restoring buildings but more importantly, in building up God's kingdom of holiness, justice and peace in your native land.

It Is All Gratuitousness

Meeting with Priests, Religious, and Seminarians

National Marian Shrine of "El Quinche,"
Quito (Ecuador), July 8, 2015

Women and men religious, priests and seminarians, I ask you to retrace your steps back to the time God gratuitously chose you. You did not buy a ticket to enter the seminary, to enter consecrated life. You were not worthy. If some religious brother, priest, seminarian or nun here today thinks that they merited this, raise your hands. It is all gratuitousness. And the entire life of a religious brother and sister, priest and seminarian must walk that path, and here why not add bishops as well. It is the path that leads to gratuitousness, the path we must follow each day: "Lord, today I did this, I did this thing well, I had this difficulty, all this but . . . all is from you, all is free gift." That is gratuitousness. We are those who receive God's gratuitousness. If we forget this, then slowly we begin to see ourselves as more important: "Look at these works you are doing," or, "Look at how they made this man a bishop of such and such a place . . . how important," or, "This man they made a Monsignor," and so on. With this way of thinking we gradually move away from what is fundamental, what Mary never moved away from: God's gratuitousness. . . .

So my advice as a brother and a father is this: remember this gratuitousness every evening. "Let it be done; thank you, because everything has been given to me by you."

A second thing that I would like to tell you is to take care of your health, but above all, take care not to fall into that illness which can be dangerous, to a lesser or greater degree, for those called freely by the Lord to follow and serve him. Do not fall into *spiritual Alzheimer's*, that is, do not forget your memories, especially the memory of where you were taken from. The scene comes to mind when the Prophet Samuel is sent to anoint the king of Israel. He goes to Bethlehem, to the home of a man named Jesse who has seven or eight children, I am not sure of the number, and God tells him that among them there is one who will be king. Naturally, Samuel sees them and says, "It must be the eldest one" for he was tall, great in stature, well built, and seemed brave. . . . But the Lord says, "No, it is not him." God's way of seeing is different from the way we see. And so he looks at each of the sons in turn, and says, "No, not him." The prophet realizes that he does not know what to do, and so asks the father of the family: "Do you not have any other sons?" Jesse replies, "Yes, there is the youngest son who is tending the sheep." Samuel said, "Send for him," and he came, just a boy, probably seventeen or eighteen years old, and God says to Jesse: "This is the one." He was taken from the back of the flock. And another prophet, when God told him to act as a prophet, replied: "But who am I? One who has been taken out of the remotest part of the sheepfold." The moral is never to forget where you have been brought from. Never forget your roots.

St. Paul clearly understood the danger of forgetting one's memory. To his beloved son, the bishop Timothy, whom he ordained, Paul offered some pastoral advice; one particular piece touched Timothy's heart: "Do not forget the faith that your grandmother and mother had," that is to say, "Do not forget from where you were taken, do not forget your roots, do not consider yourself to have been promoted." Gratuitousness is a grace that cannot exist side by side with promotion, and when a priest, seminarian, religious brother or sister embarks on a career, and I am not saying a human career is evil, then they become ill with spiritual Alzheimer's and they begin to forget where they were taken from.

Two principles for you who are priests and consecrated persons: every day renew the conviction that everything is a gift, the conviction that your being chosen is gratuitousness—we do not merit it—and every day ask for the grace not to forget your memories, and not to fall into self-importance. . . . And these two principles, if you live them each day—which entails a daily effort to remember these two principles and to ask for grace—then those two principles, when lived, will bring you life, will help you live with two attitudes. The first is service. God chose me, he took me to himself, but why? In order to serve; and a service which is particular to me and my circumstances. It is not about having my time, having my things, I have this to do, I have to close the office, I have to bless a house, but I am tired, or there is a good soap opera on television; I say this with nuns in mind. . . . No, it is none of these but

68

rather it is service, to serve, to serve and nothing else, and to serve when we are tired, and to serve when people tire us. . . .

Service, if combined with gratuitousness leads to . . . those words of Jesus: "What you have received freely, give freely." Please, please, don't put a charge on grace; please, let our pastoral works be free. It is so repulsive when one loses this sense of gratuitousness and is transformed into . . . yes, a doer of good deeds but one who loses the sense of freely giving.

The second attitude seen in a consecrated man or woman, seen in a priest who lives this gratuitousness and shows the ability to recall the past (those principles which I spoke of earlier, gratuitousness and memory), is joy and pleasure. It is a gift of Jesus, a gift which he gives if we ask for it and if we do not forget those pillars of our priestly or consecrated life, namely the sense of gratuitousness renewed daily and the ability not to forget from where we were taken.

Witnesses to Healing and Merciful Love

Meeting with Priests, Religious, and Seminarians

Coliseum of Don Bosco College, Santa Cruz de la Sierra (Bolivia), July 9, 2015

In the Gospel of Mark we also heard the experience of another disciple, Bartimaeus, who joined the group of Jesus' followers. . . .

Walking with Jesus were his apostles, the disciples and the women who were his followers. They were at his side as he journeyed through Palestine, proclaiming the Kingdom of God. There was also a great crowd. If we translate this by stretching the words a little, we can say that alongside Jesus walked the bishops, the priests, the sisters, the seminarians, the committed lay faithful, all who followed him, listening to him, namely, the faithful people of God.

Two things about this story jump out at us and make an impression. On the one hand, there is the cry of a beggar, and on the other, the different reactions of the disciples. Let us consider the different reactions of bishops, priests, sisters, seminarians, to the cries we hear or fail to hear. It is as if the Evangelist wanted to show us the effect which Bartimaeus's cry had on people's lives, on the lives of Jesus' followers. How did they react when faced with the suffering of that man on the side of the road, who no one takes any notice of, who receives no more than a gesture of almsgiving, who is wallowing in his misery and who is not part of the group following the Lord?

There were three responses to the cry of the blind man and today these three responses are also relevant. We can describe them with three phrases taken from the Gospel: "pass by," "be quiet," "take heart and get up."

1. "They passed by." Some of those who passed by did not even hear his shouting. They were with Jesus, they looked at Jesus, they wanted to hear him. But they were not listening. Passing by is the response of indifference, of avoiding other people's problems because they do not

70

affect us. It is not my problem. We do not hear them, we do not recognize them. Deafness. Here we have the temptation to see suffering as something natural, to take injustice for granted. And yes, there are people like that: I am here with God, with my consecrated life, chosen by God for ministry and yes, it is normal that there are those who are sick, poor, suffering, and it is so normal that I no longer notice the cry for help. To become accustomed. We say to ourselves, "This is nothing unusual; things were always like this, as long as it does not affect me." It is the response born of a blind, closed heart, a heart which has lost the ability to be touched and hence the possibility to change. How many of us followers of Christ run the risk of losing our ability to be astonished, even with the Lord? That wonder we had on the first encounter seems to diminish, and it can happen to anyone. Indeed it happened to the first Pope: "Whom shall we go to Lord? You have the words of eternal life." And then they betray him, they deny him, the wonder fades away. It happens when we get accustomed to things. The heart is blinded. A heart used to passing by without letting itself be touched; a life which passes from one thing to the next, without ever sinking roots in the lives of the people around us, simply because it is part of the elite who follow the Lord.

We could call this "the spirituality of zapping." It is always on the move, but it has nothing to show for it. There are people who keep up with the latest news, the most recent best sellers, but they never manage to connect with others, to strike up a relationship, to get involved, even with the Lord whom they follow, because their deafness gets worse.

You may say to me, "But those people in the Gospel were following the Master, they were busy listening to his words. They were intent on him." I think that this is one of the most challenging things about Christian spirituality. The Evangelist John tells us, "How can you love God, whom you do not see, if you do not love your brother whom you do see?" (1 Jn 4:20). They believed that they were listening to the Master, but they also made their own interpretation, and the words of the Master are distilled by their blinded hearts. One of the great temptations we encounter on the path as we follow Jesus is to separate these two things, listening to God and listening to our brothers and sisters, both of which belong together. We need to be aware of this. The way we listen to God the Father is how we should listen to his faithful people. If we do not listen in the same way, with the same heart, then something has gone wrong.

To pass by, without hearing the pain of our people, without sinking roots in their lives and in their world, is like listening to the word of God without letting it take root and bear fruit in our hearts. Like a tree, a life without roots is one which withers and dies.

2. The second phrase: "Be quiet." This is the second response to Bartimaeus's cry: "Keep quiet, don't bother us, leave us alone, for we are praying as a community, we are in a heightened state of spirituality. Don't bother us." Unlike the first response, this one hears, acknowledges, and makes contact with the cry of another person. It recognizes that he or she is there, but reacts simply by scolding. It is the bishops, priests, sisters, popes, who point their finger threateningly. In Argentina we say of teachers who point their fingers in this way: "This is like the teacher from the time of the Yrigoyen who used particularly strict methods." And the poor faithful people of God, how often are they tested, either by the bad temper or the personal situation of a follower of Christ. It is the attitude of some leaders of God's people; they continually scold others, hurl reproaches at them, tell them to be quiet. Please embrace them, listen to them, tell them that Jesus loves them. "No, you can't do that." "Madam, take your crying child out of the church as I am preaching." As if the cries of a child were not a sublime homily.

This is the drama of the isolated consciousness, of those disciples who think that the life of Jesus is only for those who deserve it. There is an underlying contempt for the faithful people of God: "This blind man who has to interfere with everything, let him stay where he is." They seem to believe there is only room for the "worthy," for the "better people," and little by little they separate themselves, become distinct, from the others. They have made their identity a badge of superiority. That identity which makes itself superior, is no longer proper to the pastor but rather to a foreman: "I made it here, now you wait in line." Such persons no longer listen; they look, but they cannot see. Let me tell you an anecdote, something I experienced around 1975 in your Archdiocese. I had made a promise to *Nuestro Señor de los Milagros* to go to Salta on pilgrimage every year if he blessed us with forty novices. He sent forty-one. After a concelebrated Mass—as at all important sanctuaries, there were many Masses, confessions, and you don't stop—I was walking up with a another priest who was with me and had come with me, and a lady came up to us, almost at the top, with an image of a saint. She was a simple woman, maybe from Salta itself, or perhaps she had come from another place, as so often happens when people take a few days to reach the capital for the Feast of the Lord of Miracles. She said to the priest who was accompanying me, "Father, please bless this image." He replied, "Lady, you were at Mass." "Yes, Father." "Well then, the blessing of God, the presence of God there blesses everything." "Yes Father, Yes Father," came the reply. At that moment another priest came up, a friend of the priest that had just spoken, but they hadn't seen each other so he says, "Oh, you're here!" He turned away and the woman—I do not know her name, we'll call her the "Yes Father Lady"—looked at me and said: "Father, please bless it." Those who always put up barriers between themselves and the people of God, push them away. They hear, but they don't listen. They deliver a sermon, but look without seeing. The need to show that they are different has closed their heart. Their need to tell themselves, consciously or subconsciously, "I am not like that person, like those people," not only cuts them off from the cry of their people, from their tears, but most of all from their reasons for rejoicing. Laughing with those who laugh, weeping with those who weep; all this is part of the mystery of a priestly heart and the heart of a consecrated person. Sometimes there are elite groups that are created by not listening and seeing, and we distance ourselves. In Ecuador, I told the priests and religious sisters present, to please ask for the grace of remembering, to never forget the memories of where they were taken from. They were called from the back of the sheepfold. Never forget, never deny your roots, don't reject that culture where you learnt from your people just because you now have a more sophisticated, important culture. There are priests who are embarrassed to speak in the native language and so they forget their Quechua, Aymara, Guarani: "No, no, I now speak well." The grace to not lose the memory of the faithful people. It is a grace. In the Book of Deuteronomy, how many times does God say to his People, "Do not forget, do not forget, do not forget." And Paul, to his beloved disciple Timothy whom he ordained, says, "Remember your mother and grandmother."

3. The third word: "Take heart and get up." This is the third response. It is not so much a direct response to the cry of Bartimaeus as a

reaction of people who saw how Jesus responded to the pleading of the blind beggar. In other words, those who gave no importance to the beggar, those who did not let him pass, or those who told him to be quiet . . . when they see Jesus' reaction they change their attitude: "Get up, he is calling you." In those who told him to take heart and get up, the beggar's cry issued in a word, an invitation, a new and changed way of responding to God's holy and faithful People.

Unlike those who simply passed by, the Gospel says that Jesus stopped and asked what was happening. "What is happening here?" "Who is making noise?" He stopped when someone cried out to him. Jesus singled him out from the nameless crowd and got involved in his life. And far from ordering him to keep quiet, he asked him, "Tell me, what do you want me to do for you?" Jesus didn't have to show that he was different, somehow apart, and he didn't give the beggar a sermon; he didn't decide whether Bartimaeus was worthy or not before speaking to him. He simply asked him a question, looked at him and sought to come into his life, to share his lot. And by doing this he gradually restored the man's lost dignity, the man who was on the side of the path and blind; Jesus included him. Far from looking down on him, Jesus was moved to identify with the man's problems and thus to show the transforming power of mercy. There can be no compassion—and I mean compassion and not pity—without stopping. If you do not stop, you do not suffer with him, you do not have divine compassion. There is no "com-passion" that does not listen and show solidarity with the other. Compassion is not about zapping, it is not about silencing pain, it is about the logic of love, of suffering with. A logic, a way of thinking and feeling, which is not grounded in fear but in the freedom born of love and of desire to put the good of others before all else. A logic born of not being afraid to draw near to the pain of our people. Even if often this means no more than standing at their side and praying with them.

This is the logic of discipleship, it is what the Holy Spirit does with us and in us. We are witnesses of this. One day Jesus saw us on the side of the road, wallowing in our own pain and misery, our indifference. Each one knows his or her past. He did not close his ear to our cries. He stopped, drew near and asked what he could do for us. And thanks to many witnesses, who told us, "Take heart; get up," gradually we experienced this merciful love, this transforming love, which enabled us to see

74

the light. We are witnesses not of an ideology, of a recipe, of a particular theology. We are not witnesses of that. We are witnesses to the healing and merciful love of Jesus. We are witnesses of his working in the lives of our communities.

And this is the pedagogy of the Master, this is the pedagogy which God uses with his people. It leads us to passing from distracted zapping to the point where we can say to others: "Take heart; get up. The Master is calling you" (Mk 10:49). Not so that we can be special, not so that we can be better than others, not so that we can be God's functionaries, but only because we are grateful witnesses to the mercy which changed us. When we live like this, there is joy and delight, and we can identify ourselves with the testimony given by the religious sister who made her own St. Augustine's counsel, "Sing and walk." This is the joy that comes from witnessing to the mercy that transforms.

On this journey we are not alone. We help one another by our example and by our prayers. We are surrounded by a cloud of witnesses (cf. Heb 12:1). . . . These women, and so many other anonymous persons, from the crowd, from the ones like us who follow Jesus, are an encouragement on our journey. That cloud of witnesses! May we press forward with the help and cooperation of all. For the Lord wants to use us to make his light reach to every corner of our world.

Perfect Like the Great Shepherd of the Sheep

Celebration of Vespers with Bishops, Priests, Deacons, Religious, Seminarians, and Catholic Movements

Metropolitan Cathedral of the Assumption, Asunción (Paraguay), July 11, 2015

Union with Jesus deepens our Christian vocation, which is concerned with what Jesus "does"—which is something much greater than mere "activities"—with becoming more like him in all that we do. The beauty of the ecclesial community is born of this union of each of her members to the person of Jesus, creating an "ensemble of vocations" in the richness of harmonic diversity. . . .

It is always good to grow in this awareness that apostolic work is carried out in communion! It is admirable to see you cooperating pastorally, with respect for the nature and ecclesial role of each of the vocations and charisms. I want to encourage all of you, priests, men and women religious, laity and seminarians, bishops, to be committed to this ecclesial collaboration, especially with regard to diocesan pastoral plans and the continental mission, and to work together with complete availability in the service of the common good. If our divisions lead to barrenness (cf. *Evangelii Gaudium*, nos. 98-101), then there is no doubt that communion and harmony lead to fruitfulness, because they are deeply attuned to the Holy Spirit.

Each of us has his or her limitations, and no one is able to reproduce Jesus in all his fullness. Although all vocations are associated with certain aspects of the life and work of Jesus, some vocations are more general and essential. Just now we praised the Lord for "he did not regard equality with God as something to be exploited" (Phil 2:6). This is the case with every Christian vocation, not regarding "equality with God as something to be exploited." A person called by God does not show off;

he or she does not seek recognition or applause; he or she does not claim to be better than others, standing apart as if on a pedestal.

Christ's supremacy is clearly described in the liturgy of the Letter to the Hebrews. As we just read from the final part of that Letter, we are to become perfect like "the great Shepherd of the sheep." And this means that all consecrated persons are to be conformed to Jesus, who in his earthly life, "with prayers and supplications, with loud cries and tears" achieved perfection when, through suffering, he learned the meaning of obedience. This too is part of the calling.

Do Not Be Afraid of Poverty and of Mercy

Celebration of Vespers with Priests,
Consecrated Men and Women, and Seminarians

Cathedral, Havana (Cuba), September 20, 2015

Cardinal Jaime spoke to us about poverty and Sr. Yaileny [Sr. Yaileny Ponce Torres, DC] spoke to us about the little ones: "They are all children." I had prepared a homily to give now, based on the biblical texts, but when prophets speak—every priest is a prophet, all the baptized are prophets, every consecrated person is a prophet—then we should listen to them. So I'm going to give the homily to Cardinal Jaime so that he can get it to you and you can make it known. Later you can meditate on it. And now let's talk a little about what these two prophets said.

Cardinal Jaime happened to say a very uncomfortable word, an extremely uncomfortable word, one which goes against the whole "cultural" structure of our world. He said "poverty," and he repeated it several times. I think the Lord wanted us to keep hearing it, and to receive it in our hearts. The spirit of the world doesn't know this word, doesn't like it, hides it—not for shame, but for scorn. . . .

It is our duty to know how to administer our goods, for they are a gift from God. But when these goods enter your heart and begin to take over your life, that's where you can get lost. Then you are no longer like Jesus. Then you have your security where the sad young man had his, the one who went away sad.

For you, priests, consecrated men and women, I think what St. Ignatius said could be useful to you (and this is not just family propaganda here!). He said that poverty was the wall and the mother of consecrated life; the "mother" because it gives birth to greater confidence in God, and the "wall" because it protects us from all worldliness. How many ruined souls there are! Generous souls, like that of the sad young man: they started out well, then gradually became attached to the love of this wealthy worldliness and ended up badly. They ended up mediocre. They ended up without love because wealth impoverishes us, in a bad way. It takes away the best that we have, and strips us of the only wealth which is truly worthwhile, so that we put our security in something else.

The spirit of poverty, the spirit of detachment, the spirit of leaving everything behind in order to follow Jesus. This leaving everything is not something I am inventing. It appears frequently in the Gospel. In the calling of the first ones who left their boat, their nets, and followed him. Those who left everything to follow Jesus.

A wise old priest once told me about what happens when the spirit of wealth, of wealthy worldliness enters the heart of a consecrated man or woman, a priest or bishop, or even a Pope—anyone. He said that when we start to save up money to ensure our future—isn't this true?—then our future is not in Jesus, but in a kind of spiritual insurance company which we manage. When, for example, a religious congregation begins to gather money and save, God is so good that he sends them a terrible bursar who brings them to bankruptcy. Such terrible bursars are some of the greatest blessings God grants his Church, because they make her free, they make her poor. Our Holy Mother the Church is poor; God wants her poor as he wanted our Holy Mother Mary to be poor.

So love poverty, like a mother. . . .

"Father, I'm not a nun. I don't take care of sick people. I'm a priest, and I have a parish, or I assist the pastor of a parish. Who is my beloved Jesus? Who is the little one? Who shows me most the mercy of the Father? Where must I find him or her?" Obviously I continue following the sequence of Matthew 25; there you have all of them: the hungry, the imprisoned, the sick—there you will meet them. But there is a special place for the priest, where the last, the least and the littlest is found—and that is in the confessional. And there, when this man or this woman shows you their misery, take care, because it is the same misery as yours, the misery from which God saved you. Is that the case? When they reveal their misery to you, please don't give them a hard time. Don't scold them or punish them. If you are without sin, you can throw the first stone. But only then. Otherwise, think about your own sins; think that you could be that person. Think that you could potentially fall even lower, and think that in this moment you hold in your hands a treasure, which is the Father's mercy. Please—I'm speaking to the priests—never tire of forgiving. Be forgivers. Like Jesus, never tire of forgiving. Don't hide behind fear or inflexibility. . . .

Brother priest, brother bishop, do not be afraid of mercy. Let it flow through your hands and through your forgiving embrace, for the man or woman before you is one of the little ones. They are Jesus.

Gratitude and Hard Work

Vespers with Priests and Religious

Cathedral of St. Patrick, New York,
September 24, 2015

This evening, my brothers and sisters, I have come to join you—priests and men and women of consecrated life—in praying that our vocations will continue to build up the great edifice of God's Kingdom in this country. I know that, as a presbyterate in the midst of God's people, you suffered greatly in the not distant past by having to bear the shame of some of your brothers who harmed and scandalized the Church in the most vulnerable of her members. . . . In the words of the Book of Revelation, I say that you "have come forth from the great tribulation" (Rev 7:14). I accompany you at this moment of pain and difficulty, and I thank God for your faithful service to his people. In the hope of helping you to persevere on the path of fidelity to Jesus Christ, I would like to offer two brief reflections.

The first concerns *the spirit of gratitude.* The joy of men and women who love God attracts others to him; priests and religious are called to find and radiate lasting satisfaction in their vocation. Joy springs from a grateful heart. Truly, we have received much, so many graces, so many blessings, and we rejoice in this. It will do us good to think back on our lives with the grace of remembrance. Remembrance of when we were first called, remembrance of the road travelled, remembrance of graces received . . . and, above all, remembrance of our encounter with Jesus Christ so often along the way. Remembrance of the amazement which our encounter with Jesus Christ awakens in our hearts. My brothers and sisters, men and women of consecrated life, and priests! Let us seek the grace of remembrance so as to grow in the spirit of gratitude. Let us ask ourselves: Are we good at counting our blessings, or have we forgotten them?

A second area is *the spirit of hard work.* A grateful heart is spontaneously impelled to serve the Lord and to find expression in a life of commitment to our work. Once we come to realize how much God has given us, a life of self-sacrifice, of working for him and for others, becomes a privileged way of responding to his great love.

Yet, if we are honest, we know how easily this spirit of generous self-sacrifice can be dampened. There are a couple of ways that this can happen; both ways are examples of that "spiritual worldliness" which weakens our commitment as men and women of consecrated life to serve, and diminishes the wonder, the amazement, of our first encounter with Christ.

We can get caught up measuring the value of our apostolic works by the standards of efficiency, good management and outward success which govern the business world. Not that these things are unimportant! We have been entrusted with a great responsibility, and God's people rightly expect accountability from us. But the true worth of our apostolate is measured by the value it has in God's eyes. To see and evaluate things from God's perspective calls for constant conversion in the first days and years of our vocation and, need I say, it calls for great humility. The cross shows us a different way of measuring success. Ours is to plant the seeds: God sees to the fruits of our labors. And if at times our efforts and works seem to fail and produce no fruit, we need to remember that we are followers of Jesus . . . and his life, humanly speaking, ended in failure, in the failure of the cross.

The other danger comes when we become jealous of our free time, when we think that surrounding ourselves with worldly comforts will help us serve better. The problem with this reasoning is that it can blunt the power of God's daily call to conversion, to encounter with him. Slowly but surely, it diminishes our spirit of sacrifice, our spirit of renunciation and hard work. It also alienates people who suffer material poverty and are forced to make greater sacrifices than ourselves, without being consecrated. Rest is needed, as are moments of leisure and self-enrichment, but we need to learn how to rest in a way that deepens our desire to serve with generosity. Closeness to the poor, the refugee, the immigrant, the sick, the exploited, the elderly living alone, prisoners and all God's other poor, will teach us a different way of resting, one which is more Christian and generous.

Gratitude and hard work: these are two pillars of the spiritual life which I have wanted, this evening, to share with you priests and religious. I thank you for prayers and work, and the daily sacrifices you make in the various areas of your apostolate. Many of these are known only to God, but they bear rich fruit for the life of the Church. . . .

I know that many of you are in the front lines in meeting the challenges of adapting to an evolving pastoral landscape. Whatever difficulties and trials you face, I ask you, like St. Peter, to be at peace and to respond to them as Christ did: he thanked the Father, took up his cross and looked forward!

Collaboration and Shared Responsibility

*Mass with Bishops, Priests, and
Religious of Pennsylvania*

*Cathedral of Sts. Peter and Paul, Philadelphia,
September 26, 2015*

One of the great challenges facing the Church in this generation is
to foster in all the faithful a sense of personal responsibility for the
Church's mission, and to enable them to fulfill that responsibility as missionary disciples, as a leaven of the Gospel in our world. This will require
creativity in adapting to changed situations, carrying forward the legacy
of the past not primarily by maintaining our structures and institutions,
which have served us well, but above all by being open to the possibilities which the Spirit opens up to us and communicating the joy of the
Gospel, daily and in every season of our life. . . .

We know that the future of the Church in a rapidly changing society
will call, and even now calls, for a much more active engagement on
the part of the laity. . . . Our challenge today is to build on those solid
foundations and to foster a sense of collaboration and shared responsibility in planning for the future of our parishes and institutions. This does
not mean relinquishing the spiritual authority with which we have been
entrusted; rather, it means discerning and employing wisely the manifold
gifts which the Spirit pours out upon the Church. In a particular way, it
means valuing the immense contribution which women, lay and religious, have made and continue to make, in the life of our communities.

The Lord Is the One Who Does the Work

Meeting with Priests, Religious, and Seminarians

Sports Field of St. Mary's School, Nairobi (Kenya), November 26, 2015

He is the one who calls, who begins, who does the work. Some people want to enter by the window. . . . It doesn't work that way. So please, if any of you have friends who came in by the window, embrace them and tell them it would be better to leave and go serve God another way, because a work which Jesus himself did not begin, by the door, will never be brought to completion. . . .

There are people who don't know why God calls them, but they know that he has. Don't worry: God will make you understand why he called you. Others want to follow the Lord for some benefit. We remember the mother of James and John, who said: "Lord, I beg you, when you cut the cake, give the biggest slice to my sons. . . . Let one of them sit at your right and the other at your left." We can be tempted to follow Jesus for ambition: ambition for money or power. All of us can say: "When I first followed Jesus, I was not like that." But it happened to other people, and little by little, they sowed it in our heart like weeds.

In our life as disciples of Jesus, there must be no room for personal ambition, for money, for worldly importance. We follow Jesus to the very last step of his earthly life: the cross. He will make sure you rise again, but you have to keep following him to the end. I tell you this in all seriousness, because the Church is not a business or an NGO. The Church is a mystery: the mystery of Jesus, who looks at each of us and says: "Follow me."

So let this be clear: Jesus is the one who calls. We have to enter by the door when he calls, not by the window; and we have to follow in his footsteps.

Obviously, when Jesus chooses us, he does not "canonize" us; we continue to be the same old sinners. If there is anyone here—a priest

85

or a religious—who doesn't think that he or she is a sinner, please raise your hand. . . . We are all sinners, starting with me. But the tenderness and love of Jesus keep us going.

"May he who began a good work in you bring it to completion." This is what keeps us going, what the love of Jesus began in us. Do you remember any time in the Gospel when the apostle James wept? Yes or no? Or when the apostle John wept? Or when any other apostle wept? The Gospel tells us that only one of the apostles wept: the one who knew that he was a sinner, so great a sinner that he betrayed his Lord. And once he realized this, he wept. . . . Then Jesus made him the Pope! Who can understand Jesus? It's a mystery!

So never stop weeping. When priests and religious no longer weep, something is wrong. We need to weep for our infidelity, to weep for the all the pain in our world, to weep for all those people who are cast aside, to weep for the elderly who are abandoned, for children who are killed, for the things we don't understand. We need to weep when people ask us: "Why?" None of us has all the answers to all those questions "why?"

A Russian writer once asked why children suffer. Whenever I see a child with cancer, a tumor or some rare disease, I too ask myself why this child has to suffer. . . . And I don't have an answer. I just look to Jesus on the cross. There are situations in life for which we can only weep, and look to Jesus on the cross. That is the only answer we have for certain injustices, certain kinds of pain, certain situations in life.

St. Paul told his disciples: "Remember Jesus Christ; remember Christ crucified." Whenever a consecrated man or woman, or a priest forgets Christ crucified, sad to say, he or she falls into an ugly sin, a sin which disgusts God, which makes God vomit. It is the sin of being tepid, lukewarm. Dear priests, sisters and brothers, religious men and women, beware of falling into the sin of tepidity.

What else can I say, from my heart to yours? I would say, never stray from Jesus. In other words, never stop praying. "But Father, sometimes it's so tiresome to pray. . . . It wearies us. It makes us fall asleep. . . ." So sleep before the Lord: that is also a way of praying, but stay there, stay there before him and pray! Don't stop praying! Once consecrated persons stop praying, their souls wither; they grow ugly, like dried figs. Ugly. The soul of a man or woman religious, or a priest who doesn't pray is an ugly soul! I'm sorry, but that's the way it is. . . .

I leave you with this question: Do I take away time from sleep, time from listening to the radio, watching television or reading the papers, in order to pray? Or would I rather do those other things? Prayer means being in the presence of God who began a good work and is bringing it to completion in each of you. . . .

The last thing I would tell you—before telling you a few other things too!—is that when we let ourselves be chosen by Jesus, it is to serve: to serve the people of God, to serve the poor, men and women who are outcasts, living on the fringes of society, to serve children and the elderly. But also to serve people who are unaware of their own pride and sin, to serve Jesus in them. Letting ourselves be chosen by Jesus means letting ourselves be chosen to serve, and not to be served.

A year or so ago, there was a gathering of priests   the nuns will get off free on this one!—and during the daily spiritual exercises one group of priests had to serve tables. Some of them complained, saying: "No! We should be served; after all, we paid, we paid to be served!" Please, let us never have any of this in the Church! To serve! Not to be served or to use other people.

That is what I wanted to say, what I felt when I heard those words of St. Paul, who trusted that the one who began a good work in you will bring it to completion at the day of Christ Jesus.

An elderly cardinal—actually, he is only a year older than I am!— once told me that when he goes to the cemetery and sees the graves of dedicated missionaries and religious, he wonders: "Why don't we canonize this or that one tomorrow," because they spent their lives in serving others. I am always moved when, after Mass, I speak with a priest or religious who tells me: "I've worked in this hospital, or with autistic children, or in the missions of the Amazon, or this or that other place for thirty or forty years." I find it very moving. That man or woman understood that following Jesus means serving others, not being served by others.

So then, I thank you very much. But you are thinking: What a rude Pope this is! He told us what to do, he beat up on us, and he never thanked us for what we do. But that is what I want to do now, the last thing I want to say, the cherry, as it were, on the cake. Thank you. I thank you for your courage in following Jesus. Thank you all the times you realize that you yourselves are sinners, and for all the tender caresses which you give to those who need them. Thank you for all those times when you helped so many people to die in peace. Thank you for "burning" your lives in hope. Thank you for letting yourselves be helped and corrected and forgiven each day.

Memory, Faithfulness, and Prayer

Meeting with Priests, Religious, and Seminarians

St. Mary's Cathedral, Kampala (Uganda), November 28, 2015

There are three things I want to tell you. First, in the book of Deuteronomy Moses keeps telling the people: "Don't forget!" And repeats this at various times throughout the book: Don't forget! Don't forget all that God has done for his people!

So the first thing I want to tell you is this: ask for, and preserve, the grace of remembrance, of memory.

. . . Don't ever forget that! That way you will keep the faith. The biggest enemy of remembrance is forgetfulness, but it is not the most dangerous one. The most dangerous enemy of remembrance is when we take for granted everything we have received, everything that has been passed down to us. . . . This is what the Church asks of you. Be witnesses like the martyrs, who gave their lives for the Gospel.

To be witnesses—and this is the second thing I want to say—we need to be faithful. Faithful to remembrance, faithful to our vocation, faithful to apostolic zeal. Fidelity means persevering on the path of holiness. . . . Fidelity means telling the bishop that you are willing to go to another diocese which needs missionaries. And that is not easy. Fidelity means persevering in our vocation. Here I think in a special way of the example of fidelity which the Sisters of the House of Charity gave me: fidelity to the poor, the sick, those in greatest need, because that is where we find Christ. . . . Remembrance means fidelity, and fidelity is only possible with prayer. Once a religious or a priest stops praying or prays too little, because he says he has too much work, he has already begun to lose his memory; she has already begun to lose her fidelity. Prayer also means humility. The humility to see our confessor regularly and to confess our sins. You cannot limp with both legs! We religious and priests cannot lead a double life. If you sin, ask God's forgiveness!

But don't keep covering up those things that God does not love, don't hide your lack of fidelity, don't put your memory in a drawer.

To Live the Anguish and the Hope of the People

Meeting with Priests, Religious, and Seminarians Gathered in the Cathedral

Sarajevo (Bosnia and Herzegovina), June 6, 2015

What does it mean, today, in Bosnia and Herzegovina, for a priest or consecrated person to serve the Lord's flock? I think it means to carry out a *pastoral ministry of hope*, caring for the sheep that are in the sheepfold, but also going out in search of those who await the Good News and who do not know where to find it, or who on their own cannot find their way to Jesus. It means to meet the people where they live, including those sheep who are outside the sheepfold, far away, who may not yet have heard of Jesus Christ. It means taking care of the formation of Catholics in their faith and in their Christian lives. Encouraging the lay faithful to be protagonists in the evangelizing mission of the Church. For this reason, I exhort you to develop Catholic communities open and "going forth," able to welcome and to encounter, and to be courageous in their evangelical witness.

The priest, the consecrated person, is called to live the anguish and the hope of the people; to work in concrete circumstances often characterized by tensions, discord, suspicions, insecurities and poverty. Faced with these painful situations, we ask God to grant us hearts that can be moved, capable of showing empathy; there is no greater witness than to be close to the spiritual and material needs of the faithful. It is the task of us bishops, priests and religious to make the people feel the nearness of God; to feel his comforting and healing hand; to be familiar with the wounds and tears of our people; to never tire of opening our hearts and offering a hand to all who ask us for help, and to all those who, perhaps because they feel ashamed, do not ask our help, but who are in great need of it. In this regard, I wish to express my deep appreciation to

Religious Sisters for everything they do with such generosity, and above all for their faithful and dedicated presence.

Dear priests, dear men and women religious, I encourage you to carry out joyfully your pastoral ministry whose effectiveness is the fruit of faith and grace, but also the fruit of a humble life, one detached from worldly concerns. Please, do not fall into the temptation of becoming a self-absorbed *élite*. The generous and transparent witness of priestly and religious life sets an example and gives encouragement to seminarians and to all those whom the Lord calls to serve him. Standing by the side of young men and women, inviting them to share experiences of service and prayer, you will help them to discover the love of Christ and to open themselves up to the call of the Lord. May the People of God see in you that faithful and generous love which Christ has left to his disciples as a legacy.

Testify to the Closeness of God

Meeting with the Missionaries of Mercy

Regia Hall, February 9, 2016

Dear Brother Priests, good evening!

It is with great pleasure that I meet with you, before giving you the mandate to be Missionaries of Mercy. This is a particularly relevant sign because it characterizes the Jubilee, and allows the unfathomable mystery of the Father's mercy to be experienced by all the local Churches. Being a Missionary of Mercy is a responsibility that is entrusted to you, because it calls you to testify firsthand to the closeness of God and to *his* way of loving. Not our way, which is always limited and sometimes contradictory, but *his* way of loving, *his* way of forgiving, which is truly mercy. I should like to offer you a few brief reflections, so that the mandate you receive may be fulfilled in a consistent manner, and as a practical help for the many people who will approach you.

First of all I wish to remind you that in this mystery you are called to express the *motherhood of the Church*. The Church is Mother because she always generates new children in the faith; the Church is Mother because she nourishes the faith; and the Church is Mother also because she offers God's forgiveness, regenerating a new life, the fruit of conversion. We cannot run the risk that a penitent not perceive the maternal presence of the Church, which welcomes and loves each one. Should this perception fail, due to our rigidity, it would do serious harm in the first place to the faith itself, because it would impede the penitent from feeling included in the Body of Christ. Moreover, it would greatly limit the penitent's sense of belonging to a community. Instead, we are called to be the living expression of the Church which as mother welcomes whosoever approaches her, conscious that through the Church one is joined to Christ. Entering the confessional, let us always remember that it is Christ who welcomes, it is Christ who listens, it is Christ who forgives, it is Christ who grants peace. We are his ministers; and we are always the first to be in need of being forgiven by him. Therefore, whatever sin may be confessed—or if the person dare not voice it, but makes it understood, it is sufficient—every missionary is called to remember his own existence as a sinner and to humbly act as a "channel" of God's mercy. I admit to you as a brother that the memory of that confession on September 21, 1953, which redirected my life, is a source of joy for me. What did that priest tell me? I don't recall. I remember only that he smiled at me, then I do not know what happened. But he welcomed me like a father.

Another important aspect is that of being able to perceive the *desire for forgiveness* present in the heart of the penitent. This desire is the fruit of the grace of God's action in people's lives, which allows them to feel nostalgia for him, for his love and for his house. Let us not forget that this very desire is at the start of conversion. The heart turns to God acknowledging the evil committed, but with the hope of obtaining forgiveness. This desire is reinforced when we decide in our own hearts to change our lives and want to sin no more. It is the moment in which we entrust ourselves to the mercy of God, and have full trust in being understood, forgiven and supported by him. Let us give great space to this desire for God and for his forgiveness; let us help it to emerge as the true expression of the grace of the Spirit which impels the conversion of heart. Here I ask you to understand not only the language of words, but also that of gestures. Should someone come to you, feeling that he must unburden himself of something, but perhaps is unable to say it, but you understand . . . and that is all right, express it this way, with a welcoming gesture. That is the first condition. The second is, that he is contrite. If a person comes to you it is because he does not want to fall into these situations, but dares not say it, is afraid to say it and then cannot. But if you do not make him do so, *ad impossibilia nemo tenetur*. The Lord understands these things, the language of gestures. Arms wide open, in order to understand what is inside that heart that cannot be said, or is said in such a way . . . a bit shamefaced . . . you understand. Receive everyone with the language by which they are able to communicate.

Lastly, I would like to recall an aspect which is seldom mentioned, but which instead is determinant: *shame*. It is not easy to place ourselves before another man, especially knowing that he represents God, and confess our sins. We feel ashamed both of what we have done and of having to confess it to another. Shame is an intimate feeling which influences our personal life and requires the confessor to assume an attitude of respect and encouragement. So often shame silences us. . . . Gestures, gestures speak. From the very first pages the Bible speaks of shame. After the sin of Adam and Eve, the sacred author immediately noted: "Then the eyes of both were opened, and they knew that they were naked; and they sewed fig leaves together and made themselves aprons" (Gn 3:7). The first reaction of this shame is that of hiding themselves from God (cf. Gn 3:8-10).

There is also another passage of Genesis which strikes me, and it is the story of Noah. We all know it, but we rarely recall the episode in which he becomes drunk. In the Bible Noah is considered a just man; even though he is not without sin: his drunkenness helps us understand how weak even he was, to the point of failing in his own dignity, a fact which Scripture expresses with the image of nakedness. Two of his sons, however, take his garment and cover him so as to restore his fatherly dignity (cf. Gn 9:18-23).

This passage makes me think of how important our role is in the confessional. Before us is a person who is "naked," and also a person who is unable to speak and does not know what to say, with his weaknesses and his limitations, with the shame of being a sinner, who is often unable to express it. Let us not forget: *before us is not a sin, but a contrite sinner*, a sinner who does not want to be like this but who cannot help it. A person who is anxious to be heard and forgiven. A sinner who promises to no longer want to be separated from the Father's house and who, with the little strength he or she can muster, wants do everything possible to live as a child of God. Thus, we are not called to judge, with a sense of superiority, as if we were immune from sin; on the contrary, we are called to act like Shem and Japheth, the sons of Noah, who took a garment to shield their father from shame. Being a confessor in accordance with the heart of Christ is the equivalent of shielding sinners with the *garment of mercy*, so they may no longer be ashamed and may recover the joy of their filial dignity, and may also know where to find it.

It is not, therefore, with the sword of judgment that we will manage to lead the lost sheep back to the fold, but with the holiness of life that is the principle of renewal and reform in the Church. Holiness is nourished with love and is able to bear the burden of those who are weakest. A Missionary of Mercy remembers to bear the sinner on his own shoulders, and to console him or her with the strength of compassion.

The sinner who goes to confession, the person who goes there, finds a father. You have heard, as have I, many people who say: "No, I never go, because I went once, ant the priest lambasted me, he really scolded me, or I went and he asked me rather obscure questions, out of curiosity." Please, this is not the good shepherd, this is the judge who perhaps believes he has not sinned, or the poor sick man who asks questions out of curiosity. I like to tell confessors: if you do not feel you are a father, do not enter the confessional, it's better, do something else. Because so much harm can be done, so much harm to a soul that is not welcomed with a father's heart, with the heart of Mother Church. Several months ago I was speaking with a wise Cardinal of the Roman Curia about the questions that some priests ask when hearing confession, and he told me: "When people start and I see that they want to unburden themselves, and I realize that I understand it, I tell them: I understand! Stay calm!" So go ahead. This is a father.

I accompany you on this missionary adventure, giving you as examples two holy ministers of God's forgiveness, St. Leopold and St. Pio. There, among the Italians there is a Capuchin who really resembles St. Leopold: small, bearded . . . , along with so many holy priests who in their lives have testified to the mercy of God. They will help you. When you feel the burden of the sins confessed to you, and that of your personal limitations and those of your words, trust in the strength of mercy that comes to meet everyone as the love which knows no bounds. And say, like so many holy confessors: "Lord, I forgive, put it on my account!" And go ahead. May the Mother of Mercy assist you and protect you in this most valuable service. May my blessing go with you; and please, do not forget to pray for me. Thank you.

Praying Is Learned, Just Like Life

Mass with Priests, Religious, Consecrated,
and Seminarians

"Venustiano Carranza" Stadium, Morelia (Mexico),
February 16, 2016

There is a saying among us which goes: "Tell me how you pray, and I will tell you how you live; tell me how you live and I will tell you how you pray. Because showing me how you pray, I will learn to find the God for whom you live, and showing me how you live, I will learn to believe in the God to whom you pray." For our life speaks of prayer and prayer speaks of our life. Praying is something learned, just as we learn to walk, to speak, to listen. The school of prayer is the school of life and in the school of life we progress in the school of prayer.

Paul said to his favorite disciple Timothy, while teaching or encouraging him to live the faith: "Remember your mother and your grandmother." And seminarians, when entering seminary, often used to tell me: "Father, I would like to have deeper mental prayer." "Look, you carry on praying as they taught you to at home and then later, little by little, your prayer will mature, just as you grew up." Praying is something learned, just like life.

Jesus wished to introduce his companions into the mystery of Life, into the mystery of His life. He showed them by eating, sleeping, curing, preaching and praying, what it means to be Son of God. He invited them to share his life, his interiority, and in his presence among them he allowed them to touch, in his flesh, the life of the Father. He helped them to experience, in his gaze, in his going out in power, the newness of saying "Our Father." In Jesus this expression "Our Father" has no trace of routine or mere repetition. On the contrary, it contains a sense of life, of experience, of authenticity. With these two words, "Our Father," he knew how to live praying and to pray living.

Jesus invites us to do the same. Our first call is to experience this merciful love of the Father in our lives, in our experiences. His first call

97

is to introduce us into the new dynamic of love, of sonship. Our first calling is to learn to say, "Our Father," as Paul insists: *Abba*.

"Woe to me if I do not preach the Gospel!" says St. Paul, "Woe to me!" For to evangelize, he continues, is not a cause for glory but rather a need (1 Cor 9:16).

He has invited us to share in his life, his divine life, and woe to us consecrated men and women, seminarians, priests, bishops, woe to us if we do not share it, woe to us if we are not witnesses to what we have seen and heard, woe to us. We do not want to be "administrators of the divine," we are not and do not want to be employees in God's firm, for we are invited to share in his life, we are invited to enter into his heart, a heart that prays and lives, saying, "Our Father." What is our mission if not to say with our lives—from the beginning to the end, as our brother bishop who died last night—what is our mission if not to say with our entire lives, "Our Father"?

He who is Our Father, it is he to whom we pray every day with insistence. And what do we tell him in one of the petitions of that prayer? Lead us not into temptation. Jesus himself did the same thing. He prayed that his disciples—yesterday's and today's—would not fall into temptation. What could be one of the sins which besets us? What could be one of the temptations which springs up not only in contemplating reality but also in living it? What temptation can come to us from places often dominated by violence, corruption, drug trafficking, disregard for human dignity, and indifference in the face of suffering and vulnerability? What temptation might we suffer over and over again—we who are called to the consecrated life, to the presbyterate, to the episcopate—what temptation might we endure in the face of all this, in the face of this reality which seems to have become a permanent system?

I think that we could sum it up in a single word: "resignation." And faced with this reality, the devil can overcome us with one of his favorite weapons: resignation. "And what are you going to do about it? Life is like that." A resignation which paralyzes us and prevents us not only from walking, but also from making the journey; a resignation which not only terrifies us, but which also entrenches us in our "sacristies" and false securities; a resignation which not only prevents us from proclaiming, but also inhibits our giving praise and takes away the joy, the joy of giving praise. A resignation which not only hinders our looking to the future, but also stifles our desire to take risks and to change. And so, "Our Father, lead us not into temptation."

How good it is for us to tap into our memories when we are tempted. How much it helps us to look at the "stuff" of which we are made. It did not all begin with us, nor will it all end with us, and so it does us good to look back at our past experiences which have brought us to the present.

And in this remembering, we cannot overlook someone who loved this place so much, who made himself a son of this land. We cannot overlook that person who could say of himself: "They took me from the tribunal and put me in charge of the priesthood for my sins. Me, useless and quite unable to carry out such a great undertaking; me, who didn't know how to use an oar, they chose me to be the first Bishop of Michoacán" (Vasco Vázquez de Quiroga, *Pastoral Letter*, 1554). I wish to add here my thanks to the Cardinal Archbishop who had the idea of me celebrating this Mass with the pastoral staff and the chalice that belonged to the first Bishop.

With you, I would like to recall this evangelizer, first known as "the Spaniard who became an Indian."

The situation of the Purhépechas Indians, whom he described as being "sold, humiliated, and homeless in marketplaces, picking up scraps of bread from the ground," far from tempting him to listless resignation, succeeded in kindling his faith, strengthening his compassion and inspiring him to carry out plans that were a "breath of fresh air" in the midst of so much paralyzing injustice. The pain and suffering of his brothers and sisters became his prayer, and his prayer led to his response. And among the Indians, he was known as "Tata Vasco," which in the Purhépechan language means, father, dad, tata, daddy. . . .

It is to this prayer, to this expression, that Jesus calls us.

Father, dad, daddy . . . lead us not into the temptation of resignation, lead us not into the temptation of falling into sloth, lead us not into the temptation of losing our memory, lead us not into the temptation of forgetting our elders who taught us by their lives to say, "Our Father."

The Book of Our Life as a Living Gospel

Apostolic Journey to Poland on the Occasion of the Thirty-First World Youth Day, Mass with Priests, Men and Women Religious, Consecrated People, and Polish Seminarians

St. John Paul II Shrine, Kraków, Poland, July 30, 2016

The words of the Gospel we have just heard (cf. Jn 20:19-31) speak to us of *a place, a disciple* and *a book*.

The *place* is where the disciples gathered on the evening of Easter; we read only that its doors were closed (cf. v. 19). Eight days later, the disciples were once more gathered there, and the doors were still shut (cf. v. 26). Jesus enters, stands *in their midst* and brings them his peace, the Holy Spirit and the forgiveness of sins: in a word, God's mercy. Behind those closed doors there resounds Jesus' call to his followers: "As the Father has sent me, so I send you" (v. 21).

Jesus *sends*. From the beginning, he wants his to be a Church on the move, a Church that *goes out* into the world. And he wants it to do this just as he did. He was not sent into the world by the Father to wield power, but to take the form of a slave (cf. Phil 2:7); he came not "to be served, but to serve" (Mk 10:45) and to bring the Good News (cf. Lk 4:18). In the same way, his followers are sent forth in every age. The contrast is striking: whereas the disciples had closed the doors out of fear, Jesus sends them out on mission. He wants them to open the doors and go out to spread God's pardon and peace, with the power of the Holy Spirit.

This call is also addressed to us. How can we fail to hear its echo in the great appeal of St. John Paul II: "Open the doors"? Yet, in our lives as priests and consecrated persons, we can often be tempted to remain enclosed, out of fear or convenience, within ourselves and in our surroundings. But Jesus directs us to a one-way street: that of going forth from ourselves. It is a one-way trip, with no return ticket. It involves making an exodus from ourselves, losing our lives for his sake (cf. Mk 8:35) and setting out on the path of self-gift. Nor does Jesus like journeys made halfway, doors half-closed, lives lived on two tracks. He asks us to pack lightly for the journey, to set out renouncing our own security, with him alone as our strength.

In other words, the life of Jesus' closest disciples, which is what we are called to be, is shaped by *concrete love*, a love, in other words, marked by *service* and *availability*. It is a life that has no closed spaces or private property for our own use, or at least there shouldn't be. Those who choose to model their entire life on Jesus no longer choose their own places; they go where they are sent, in ready response to the one who calls. They do not even choose their own times. The house where they live does not belong to them, because the Church and the world are the open spaces of their mission. Their wealth is to put the Lord *in the midst* of their lives and to seek nothing else for themselves. So they flee the satisfaction of being at the center of things; they do not build on the shaky foundations of worldly power, or settle into the comforts that compromise evangelization. They do not waste time planning a secure future, lest they risk becoming isolated and gloomy, enclosed within the narrow walls of a joyless and desperate self-centeredness. Finding their happiness in the Lord, they are not content with a life of mediocrity, but burn with the desire to bear witness and reach out to others. They love to take risks and to set out, not limited to trails already blazed, but open and faithful to the paths pointed out by the Spirit. Rather than just getting by, they rejoice to evangelize.

Secondly, today's Gospel presents us with the one *disciple* who is named: Thomas. In his hesitation and his efforts to understand, this disciple, albeit somewhat stubborn, is a bit like us and we find him likeable. Without knowing it, he gives us a great gift: he brings us closer to God, because God does not hide from those who seek him. Jesus shows Thomas his glorious wounds; he makes him touch with his hand the infinite tenderness of God, the vivid signs of how much he suffered out of love for humanity.

For us who are disciples, it is important to put our humanity in contact with the flesh of the Lord, to bring to him, with complete trust and utter sincerity, our whole being. As Jesus told St. Faustina, he is happy when we tell him everything: he is not bored with our lives, which he already knows; he waits for us to tell him even about the events of our day (cf. *Diary*, September 6, 1937). That is the way to seek God: through prayer that is transparent and unafraid to hand over to him our troubles, our struggles and our resistance. Jesus' heart is won over by sincere openness, by hearts capable of acknowledging and grieving over their weakness, yet trusting that precisely there God's mercy will be active.

What does Jesus ask of us? He desires hearts that are truly consecrated, hearts that draw life from his forgiveness in order to pour it out with compassion on our brothers and sisters. Jesus wants hearts that are open and tender towards the weak, never hearts that are hardened. He wants docile and transparent hearts that do not dissimulate before those whom the Church appoints as our guides. Disciples do not hesitate to ask questions, they have the courage to face their misgivings and bring them to the Lord, to their formators and superiors, without calculations or reticence. A faithful disciple engages in constant watchful discernment, knowing that the heart must be trained daily, beginning with the affections, to flee every form of duplicity in attitudes and in life.

The Apostle Thomas, at the conclusion of his impassioned quest, not only came to believe in the resurrection, but found in Jesus his life's greatest treasure, his Lord. He says to Jesus: "My Lord and my God!" (v. 28). We would do well, today, and every day, to pray these magnificent words, and to say to the Lord: You are my one treasure, the path I must follow, the core of my life, my all.

The final verse of today's Gospel speaks of a *book*: it is the Gospel that, we are told, does not contain all the many other signs that Jesus worked (v. 30). After the great sign of his mercy, we could say that there is no longer a need to add another. Yet one challenge does remain. There is room left for the signs needing to be worked by us, who have received the Spirit of love and are called to spread mercy. It might be said that the Gospel, the living book of God's mercy that must be continually read and reread, still has many blank pages left. It remains an open book that we are called to write in the same style, by the works of mercy we practice. Let me ask you this, dear brothers and sisters:

What are the pages of your books like? Are they blank? May the Mother of God help us in this. May she, who fully welcomed the word of God into her life (cf. Lk 8:20-21), give us the grace to be living writers of the Gospel. May our Mother of Mercy teach us how to take concrete care of the wounds of Jesus in our brothers and sisters in need, those close at hand and those far away, the sick and the migrant, because by serving those who suffer we honor the flesh of Christ. May the Virgin Mary help us to spend ourselves completely for the good of the faithful entrusted to us, and to show concern for one another as true brothers and sisters in the communion of the Church, our holy Mother.

Dear brothers and sisters, each of us holds in his or her heart a very personal page of the book of God's mercy. It is the story of our own calling, the voice of the love that attracted us and transformed our life, leading us to leave everything at his word and to follow him (cf. Lk 5:11). Today let us gratefully rekindle the memory of his call, which is stronger than any resistance and weariness on our part. As we continue this celebration of the Eucharist, the center of our lives, let us thank the Lord for having entered through our closed doors with his mercy, for calling us, like Thomas, by name, and for giving us the grace to continue writing his Gospel of love.

The Formation of Priests

Graduate Presbyters

Meeting with the Rectors and Students of the Pontifical Colleges and Residences of Rome

Paul VI Hall, May 12, 2014

Good morning, and I thank you very much for this presence. I thank Cardinal Stella for his words, and I apologize for the delay . . . .

To the 146 of you who are from countries in the Middle East, and also to some of you from Ukraine, I want to say that I am very close to you at this moment of suffering: truly, very close, and in prayer. There is so much suffering in the Church; the Church suffers so much, and the suffering Church is also the persecuted Church in some parts, and I am close to you. Thank you. And now I would like . . . There were some questions, I have seen them, but if you wish to change them or make them somewhat more spontaneous, there's no problem, do so with all liberty!

Good morning, Holy Father. My name is Daniel. I come from the United States, I am a Deacon at the North American College. We have come to Rome above all for an academic formation and to keep faith in this commitment. How do we not neglect an integral priestly formation, either at the personal or community level? Thank you.

Thank you for the question. It is true; your main purpose here is academic formation: to get a degree in this or that. . . . However, there is the danger of academicism. Yes, the bishops send you here so that you can earn a degree, but they also do so in order that you may return to the diocese. However, in dioceses you must work in the presbytery as presbyters, *graduate* presbyters. And if one falls into this danger of academicism, it isn't Father who returns but the "doctor." And this is dangerous. There are four pillars in priestly formation: I have said this so many times, perhaps you have already heard it. Four pillars: spiritual formation, academic formation, community formation and apostolic formation. It's true that here in Rome emphasis is placed—since this is why you were sent—on intellectual formation; however, the other three pillars must be cultivated, and all four interact among themselves, and I wouldn't understand a priest who comes to get a degree in Rome and does not have a community life. This is not all right. Either he is not taking care of his spiritual life—daily Mass, daily prayer, *lectio divina*, personal prayer with the Lord—or his apostolic life: on the weekend doing something, for a change of air, but also the apostolic air, doing something there. . . . It's true that study is an apostolic dimension; but it is important that the other three pillars are also looked after! Academic purism is not beneficial, it is not beneficial. And this is why I liked your question, because it gives me the opportunity to tell you these things. The Lord has called you to be priests, to be presbyters: this is the fundamental rule.

And there is something else that I would like to stress: if only the academic part is considered, there is a danger of sliding into ideologies, and this makes one sick. And it also sickens one's conception of the Church. To understand the Church, one must understand her through study but also through prayer, through community life and through apostolic life. When we slide into an ideology and go down this road, we will have a non-Christian hermeneutic, a hermeneutic of an ideological Church. And this is harmful, it is an illness. One's hermeneutic of the Church has to be the hermeneutic which the Church herself offers us, which the Church herself gives us. To perceive the Church with the eyes of a Christian; to understand the Church with the mind of a Christian; to understand the Church with the heart of a Christian; to understand the Church through Christian works. Otherwise one does not understand the Church, or understands her poorly. Therefore, yes, it is important to emphasize academic study because that is why you were sent here, but do not neglect the other three pillars: the spiritual life, community life and the apostolic life. I don't know if this answers your question. . . . Thank you.

Good morning, Holy Father. I am Thomas from China. I am a seminarian at the Collegio Urbano. Sometimes living in community isn't easy: what advice would you give us, based on your own experience, for making our community a place of human and spiritual growth and of the exercise of priestly charity?

Once, an old bishop from Latin America said: "The worst seminary is better than no seminary." If one prepares for the priesthood alone, without a community, this is harmful. The life of the seminary, that is, community life, is very important. It is very important because there is sharing among brothers who are journeying toward the priesthood; but there are also problems, there are battles: battles for power, battles over ideas, even hidden struggles; and the capital vices arise: envy, jealousy . . . And good things also arise: friendships, the exchange of ideas, and this is what is important for community life. Community life isn't paradise, it's at least purgatory—no, it's not that . . . [they laugh], but it's not paradise! A Jesuit saint said that the greatest penance for him was community life. It's true, isn't it? Therefore, I think we must go forward in community life. But how? There are four or five things that will help us a great deal. Never, never speak ill of others. If I have something against another, or if I don't agree with him: I have to tell him to his face! But we clerics are tempted not to speak to another to his face, to be too diplomatic, that clerical language. . . . However, it harms us, it harms us! I remember once, twenty-two years ago, I had just been appointed bishop and in that vicariate I had as secretary—Buenos Aires is divided into four vicariates—a young recently ordained priest. And in the first months, I did something, I took a somewhat diplomatic decision—too diplomatic—with the consequences that come from such decisions that are not taken in the Lord, no? And in the end, I said to him: "See what a problem this is, I don't know how to put it in order. . . . " And he looked at me in the face—a young man!—and he said to me: "Because you acted wrongly, you did not make a fatherly decision," and he said three or four strong things to me! He was very respectful, but he did say them to me. And then, when he left, I thought: "I will never remove him from the post of secretary: he is a true brother!" Instead, those who tell you lovely things to your face and then say not so lovely things behind your back. . . . This is important. . . . Gossip is the plague of the community; one must speak face to face, always. And if you do not have the courage to speak to someone's face, speak to the Superior or to the Director. And he will help you, but don't go to your companion's rooms and speak ill of others! They say that gossip is something women are prone to, but also men, also us! We gossip enough! And this destroys the community. Then, it is something else to hear, to listen to different opinions and to discuss opinions, but well, seeking truth, seeking unity: this helps the community. Once my spiritual father . . . I was a student of philosophy; he was a philosopher, a metaphysician, but what a good spiritual father he was . . . I went to him and the problem came out that I was angry with someone: "But I'm angry with him because of this, this and this . . . " I told my spiritual Father everything I had inside me. And he asked me only one question: "Tell me, have you prayed for him?" Nothing more. And I said: "No." He was silent. "We're done," he said to me. To pray, to pray for all the members of the community, but to pray primarily for those with whom I have a problem, or for those whom I don't love, because sometimes not loving a person is something natural, instinctive. Pray, and the Lord will do the rest. But always pray. Community prayer. These two things—I don't want to say too much—but I assure you that if you do these two things, the community will move forward, you can live well, speak well, discuss well, pray well together. Two small things: do not speak ill of others and pray for those with whom you have a problem. I could say more, but I think this is sufficient.

Good morning, Holy Father.

Good morning.

My name is Charbel, I am a seminarian from Lebanon and in formation at the Collegio Sedes Sapientiae. Before asking my question, I would like to thank you for your closeness to our people in Lebanon and in the entire Middle East. My question is this: Last year you left your country and homeland. What would you recommend to us for better managing our arrival and stay in Rome?

Well, it's different . . . your arrival in Rome and my transfer of diocese: it's somewhat different, but all right. . . . I remember the first time I left [my country] to come to study here. . . . First there is the novelty, it is the novelty of things, and we must be patient with ourselves. The beginning is like a wedding engagement: it's all beautiful, ah, the newness, the newness of things . . . ; but this should not be criticized, it's how it is! This happens to everyone; things are this way for everyone. And then, returning to one of the pillars, first comes integration into the life of the community and into the life of study, directly. I have come for this, to do this. And then finding work for the weekend, an apostolic work, is important. Do not remain closed and do not be scattered. But the early days are the time for novelties: "I would like to do this, go to that museum, to this film, or to this or that." Go ahead, don't be worried, it's normal for this to happen. But then, you have to get serious. What have I come to do? To study. Study in earnest! And take advantage of the many opportunities that this stay gives you. The newness of the universality: getting to know people from so many different places, from so many different countries, from so many different cultures. The opportunity to dialogue among yourselves. "But, what's it like in your homeland? And what's that like? And in mine it is . . ."; and this exchange does great good, great good. I think I simply wouldn't say more. Don't be scared by the joy of the novelty: it's the joy of the first engagement, before the problems begin. And go forward. Then, get serious.

Good morning, Holy Father. I am Daniel Ortiz and I am Mexican. Here in Rome I live in the Collegio Maria Mater Ecclesiae. Your Holiness, in fidelity to our vocation, we are in need of constant discernment, vigilance and personal discipline. How did you do this, when you were a seminarian, when you were a priest, when you were Bishop and now that you are Pope? And how would you advise us in this regard? Thank you.

Thank you. You said the word *vigilance*. Vigilance: this is a Christian attitude. Vigilance over oneself: What is happening in my heart? Because where my heart is, there my treasure will be. What is happening there? The Eastern Fathers say that I must know well if my heart is in turmoil or if my heart is calm. The first question: vigilance over your heart: Is it in turmoil? If it's in turmoil, you can't see what's inside. It's like the sea, no? When the sea is like this, one cannot see the fish. . . . The first piece of advice, when your heart is in turmoil, is the advice of the Russian Fathers: go beneath the mantle of the Holy Mother of God. Remember that the first Latin antiphon is exactly this: in times of turmoil, take refuge under the mantle of the Holy Mother of God. It is the antiphon "*Sub tuum presidium confugimus, Sancta Dei Genitrix*": It is the first Latin antiphon dedicated to Our Lady. It's interesting, no? Be watchful. Is there turmoil? First go there, and wait there until there is a bit of calm: through

111

prayer, through entrustment to Our Lady. . . . One of you might say to me: "But Father, in this time of such good modern advancements, of psychology, of psychiatry, in such moments of turmoil I think it would be better to go to a psychiatrist to help me. . . ." I don't rule this out, but first go to your Mother, because a priest who forgets his Mother, especially in moments of turmoil, he's missing something. He is an orphan priest: he has forgotten his mother! And it's in the difficult moments that a child always goes to his mother. And we are children in the spiritual life. Never forget this! To be watchful over the state of my heart. In times of turmoil, go to seek refuge under the mantle of the Holy Mother of God. So say the Russian monks and, in truth, so it is.

Then, what do I do? I try to understand what is happening, but always in peace—to understand in peace. Then peace returns and I can perform the *discussio conscientiae*. When I am in peace and there is no turmoil: "What happened today in my heart?" And this is *keeping watch*. Keeping watch is not a matter of entering a torture chamber, no! It is watching one's heart. We must be *masters* over our heart. What does my heart feel, what does it seek? What made me happy today, and what didn't make me happy? Do not end the day without doing this. As bishop, a question I would ask priests was: "Tell me, how do you get ready for bed?" And they didn't understand. "But what do you mean by that?" "Yes, how do you end the day?" "Oh, destroyed, Father, because there's so much work, the parish, so much. . . . Then I have a little dinner, I take a bite and go to bed, I watch TV and relax a bit." "And you don't pass by the Tabernacle first?" There are things that make us see where our heart is. Never, never—and this is vigilance!—never end the day without spending a little time there, before the Lord, to reflect and ask yourself: "What happened in my heart?" In sad moments, in happy moments: What was that sadness about? What was that joy about? This is vigilance. Keeping watch also over one's moments of depression and enthusiasm. "Today I'm down; I don't know what is happening." Keep watch: Why am I down? Perhaps you need to go to someone who can help you. . . . This is vigilance. "Oh, I'm filled with joy!" But why am I joyful today? What happened in my heart? This is no sterile introspection, no, no! This is for the purpose of knowing the state of my heart, my life, how I am walking on the path of the Lord. For if there is no vigilance, the heart goes everywhere, and the imagination follows behind: "Go, go . . . " and then one might not end up well. I like the question about vigilance. These are not ancient things of times past, we haven't gone beyond these things. They are *human* things, and like all human things, they are timeless. We always carry them with us. Keeping watch over the heart was precisely the wisdom of first Christian monks; they taught this, to keep watch over the heart.

May I make an aside? Why have I spoken about Our Lady? I recommend to you what I said earlier, seek refuge. . . . A beautiful relationship with Our Lady, a relationship with Our Lady helps us to have a good relationship with the Church: both are Mothers. . . . You know the beautiful passage of St. Isaac, Abbot of Stella: what can be said of Mary can be said of the Church and also of our soul. All three are feminine, all three are Mothers, all three give life. The relationship with Our Lady is the relationship of a son. . . . Keep watch over this: if one doesn't have a good relationship with Our Lady, there is something of an orphan in my heart. I remember once, thirty years ago, I was in Northern Europe. I had to travel there to teach at the University of Cordoba, where at the time I was Vice-Chancellor. And a family of practicing Catholics invited me to their home; the country was a bit too secularized. And at dinner—they had many children, they were practicing Catholics, both were university professors, both were also catechists—at a certain point, speaking of Jesus Christ—enthusiasts of Jesus Christ!—I am talking about thirty years ago, they said: "Yes, thank God we have gotten past the stage of Our Lady. . . ." "How so?", I said. "Yes, because we have discovered Jesus Christ, and we no longer need her." I was somewhat pained; I didn't understand well. And we spoke a little about this. This is not maturity! It is not mature. To forget one's mother is something awful. . . . To say it another way: if you don't want Our Lady as Mother, you will certainly have her as a mother-in-law! And this is not good. Thank you.

Long live Jesus, long live Mary! Thank you, Holy Father, for your words about Our Lady. My name is Don Ignacio and I come from Manila, the Philippines. I am working on my doctorate in Mariology at the Pontifical Theological Faculty Marianum, and I reside at the Philippine Pontifical College. Holy Father, my question is this: The Church needs pastors who are able to guide, govern and communicate as today's world requires us. How does one learn and exercise leadership in priestly life, taking on the model of Christ who humbled himself unto taking on the Cross, death on a Cross? Taking on the condition of servant unto death on the Cross? Thank you.

But your Bishop is a great communicator!

He is Cardinal Tagle.

Leadership . . . this is the heart of the question. . . . There is only one road—then I will speak about pastors—but for leadership there is only one road: service. There is no other way. If you have many qualities—the ability to communicate, etc.—but you are not a servant, your leadership will fail, it is useless, it has not power to gather [people] together. Only service: to be at the service. . . . I remember a very good spiritual father. People went to him, so much so that sometimes he couldn't pray the whole breviary. And, at night, he would go to the Lord and say: "Lord, I didn't do your will, or even my own! I did the will of others!" Thus the both of them—he and the Lord—consoled one another. Many times service means doing the will of others. A priest who works in a very humble district—very humble!—a *villa miseria*, a slum, said: "I would have to shut the windows, the doors, all of them, because at a certain point there are so, so many who come to ask me for this spiritual thing, this material thing, that in the end I would want to shut everything. But this is not of the Lord," he would say. It is true: you cannot lead a people where service is lacking.

The service of a pastor. A pastor must always be available to his people. A pastor must help the people to grow, to walk. Yesterday, in the Reading I was intrigued because the word "to push" was used in the Gospel. The shepherd pushes the sheep to go out and look for grass. I was intrigued: he makes them go out, he makes them go out with force! The original has this nuance: *he makes them go out* but with *force!* It's like *throwing them out*: "Go, go!" The pastor who makes his people grow and who always goes with his people. Sometimes, the pastor must go in front in order to indicate the way; at other times, must be among them to find out what is happening; and many times behind, to help those who are falling behind and also to follow the scent of the sheep that know where the good grass is. The shepherd . . . St. Augustine says, taking up Ezekiel, must be at the service of the sheep and he underlines two dangers: the shepherd who exploits the sheep in order to eat, to make money, for economic and material interests; and the shepherd who exploits the sheep to dress well. Meat and wool, St. Augustine says. Read that beautiful sermon *De Pastoribus*. We need to read and reread it. Yes, these are the two sins of pastors: money, that they become rich and do things for money—profiteer pastors. And vanity, pastors who believe they are in a superior state to their people, detached . . . let's think, prince pastors. The profiteer pastor and the prince pastor. These are the two temptations of which St. Augustine speaks in his sermon, taking up the passage of Ezekiel. It is true, a pastor who seeks himself, be it by way of money or by way of vanity, is not a servant, he has no true leadership. Humility must be the shepherd's weapon: humble, always at the service of others. He must *seek* to serve. And it's not easy to be humble; no, it's not easy! The Desert Monks say that vanity is like an onion: when you pick up an onion, and begin to peel it; and you feel vain, you begin to peel away your vanity. And you go, and go, to another layer, and another, and another, and another . . . and ultimately you arrive at . . . nothing. "Ah, thank God, I've peeled the onion, I've peeled away my vanity." Do this, and you'll smell like an onion! So say the desert Fathers. This is what vanity is like. Once I heard a Jesuit—good, he was a good man—but he was so vain, so vain. . . . And we all told him: "You're vain!" But he was so good that we all forgave him. And he went to do the Spiritual Exercises, and when he returned, he said to us, in community: "What beautiful exercises! I spent eight days in Heaven, and I discovered that I was so vain! But, thank God, I have overcome all my passions!" Vanity is like this! It is so difficult to remove vanity from a priest. The people of God will forgive you many things: they will forgive you if you have had an emotional slip, they will forgive you. However, they will not forgive you if you are a pastor attached to money, if you are a vain pastor who does not treat people well. For someone who is vain does not treat people well. Money, vanity, pride: the three steps that lead you to all the sins. The people of God understand our weaknesses, and forgive them; but these two they do not forgive! They do not forgive attachment to money in a pastor. And if they aren't treated well, they don't forgive this. It's curious, isn't it? We must battle against these two defects in order not to have them. Then, leadership must enter into service, but with a personal love for the people. I once heard about a parish priest: "That man knew the name of all the people of his district, even the names of the dogs!" It is beautiful! He was close, he knew each one, he knew the history of all the families, he knew everything. And he helped. He was so close. . . . Closeness, service, humility, poverty and sacrifice. I remember the old parish priests in Buenos Aires, when there were no mobile phones or answering machines; they slept with the telephone beside them. No one died without the Sacraments. People rang them at any hour, they got up and went. Service, service. And as Bishop, it pained me when I called a parish and the answering machine answered. . . . That's no leadership! How can you lead a people if you don't hear them, if you are not at their service? These are the things that come to me, not much . . . not well ordered, but they are meant to answer your question. . . .

Good morning, Holy Father.

Good morning.

My name is Don Sérge, I'm from Cameroon. My formation is taking place at the College of St. Paul the Apostle. Here is my question: When we return to our dioceses and communities, we will be called to new ministerial responsibilities and new formative tasks. How can all the dimensions of the ministerial life coexist in a balanced way: prayer, pastoral commitments, formational obligations, without neglecting any one of them? Thank you.

There is a question I didn't answer: it eluded me, perhaps—being irresponsible is dishonest!—and I want to connect it with this one. They were asking me: "How do you do these things as Pope?" And yours . . . I will answer yours by recounting with complete simplicity what I do, so as not to neglect anything. Prayer. In the morning I try to pray Lauds and spend a little time in prayer in *lectio divina* with the Lord. When I get up, I first read the "coded messages," and then I do this. And then, I celebrate Mass. Then the work begins: one day it's one kind of work and another day it's something else. . . . I try to do one thing at a time.

Lunch is at noon, then a little siesta. After the siesta, at three o'clock—excuse me—I say Vespers, at three. . . . If they aren't said then, they won't be said at all! There's also reading, the Office of Readings for the next day. Then afternoon work, the things I am obliged to do. . . . Then, I spend a little time in Adoration and pray the Rosary; dinner, and then I'm done. That's how it goes.

But sometimes not everything gets done, because I let myself be led by imprudent demands: too much work, or thinking that if I don't do this today, I won't do it tomorrow. . . . Adoration falls by the wayside, my siesta falls by the wayside, this or that falls by the wayside. . . . Even here one must be vigilant: you will return to your dioceses and what happens to me will happen to you: it's normal. Work, prayer, a little time for rest, get out of the house, take a walk, all of this is important . . . but you must regulate it through *vigilance* and also through good advice. . . . It is ideal to finish the day tired: this is ideal. You shouldn't need to take pills, to end tired. However, with good tiredness, not imprudent tiredness, because that's bad for one's health and, in the long run, one pays dearly for this. I look at Sandro's face, who laughs and says: "But you don't do this!" It's true. This is the ideal, but I don't always do it, because I am also a sinner, and I'm not always that organized. But this is what you should do. . . .

Good morning, Holy Father. I am Fernando Rodriguez. I am a new priest from Mexico. I was ordained one month ago, and I live at the Mexican College. Holy Father, you have reminded us that the Church is in need of a New Evangelization. In fact, in your [Apostolic Exhortation] Evangelii Gaudium, you reflected on the preparation for preaching, on the homily, and on the proclamation as a form of passionate dialogue between a pastor and his people. Can you return to this subject of the New Evangelization? Also, Your Holiness, we would like to ask you how a priest should be for the New Evangelization. What should he be like? Thank you.

It was at Santo Domingo in '92 when St. John Paul II spoke about the New Evangelization—I thought it was the first time but afterward I was told that it wasn't the first time. He said that it needs a new methodology, a new ardor, renewed apostolic zeal, and I don't remember the third.

117

. . . Who remembers it? Expression! To look for an expression that is in keeping with the singularity of the times. And for me, in the Aparecida Document it is very clear. The Aparecida Document develops this well. For me, evangelization requires going out of oneself; it requires the dimension of transcendence: the transcendent in the adoration of God, in contemplation, and transcendence toward our brothers and sisters, toward the people. To go forth, go forth! For me this is the kernel of evangelization. And going forth means going somewhere, i.e., closeness. If you don't go out of yourself you will never reach closeness! Closeness. To be close to people, to be close to everyone, to all those to whom we should be close. All people. Go forth. Closeness. One cannot evangelize without closeness! Closeness with kindness; the closeness of love, also physical closeness; to be close to another. And here you made a connection to homilies. The problem with boring homilies—so to speak—the problem with boring homilies is that there is no closeness. It is precisely in the homily that we measure a pastor's closeness to his people. If in the homily you speak, let's say, twenty, twenty-five or thirty, forty minutes— these aren't fantasies, this happens!—and you speak of abstract things, of truths of the faith, you are not delivering a homily, you are playing school! That is different! You are not close to the people. That is why the homily is important: calibrate it, get an idea of how close the priest is. I think that in general our homilies aren't good, they do not really belong to the homiletic literary genre: they are conferences, or they are lessons, or reflections. But a homily—and ask your theology professor about this—the homily at Mass, the Word of Almighty God, is a sacramental. For Luther it was almost a sacrament: it was *ex opere operato*, the Word preached; for others, it is only *ex opere operantis*. However, I think it is somewhere in the middle, a bit of both. The theology of the homily is somewhat sacramental. It is different than saying words about a topic. It's something more. It implies prayer, it implies study, it implies knowing the people to whom you will speak, it implies closeness. Regarding the homily, for evangelization to succeed we must move far ahead, we are behind. It is one of the points where today the Church stands in need of conversion: prepare our homilies so that people can understand them. And after eight minutes, one's attention span is exhausted. A homily shouldn't be longer than eight or ten minutes. It should be brief, it should be firm. I recommend two books to you; they are from my day,

118

but they are good on this aspect of preparing homilies; they will help you very much. First, *The Theology of Preaching* by Hugo Rahner. Not Karl, but Hugo. One can read Hugo easily; Karl is difficult to read. This is a jewel: *The Theology of Preaching*. And the other is that of Fr. Domenico Grasso, which introduces us to what a homily is. I think it has the same title: *Theology of Preaching*. This will help you quite a lot. Closeness, the homily. . . . There is something else I wanted to say. . . . Go forth, be close, make the homily the measure of how close I am to the People of God. And another category I like to use is that of the peripheries. When one goes forth, one shouldn't just go halfway, he has to go all the way, to the end. Some say that one has to begin evangelizing with those who are furthest away, as the Lord did. This is what comes to me to say about your question. This matter of the homily is true: for me it is one of the problems which the Church needs to study and be converted. Homilies, homilies: they are not school lessons, they are not conferences, they are something else. I like it when priests get together for two hours to prepare the coming Sunday's homily, because it gives them an atmosphere of prayer, of study, of exchange of opinions. This is good, it is very beneficial. Preparing it together with someone else is very good.

Praised be Jesus Christ! My name is Voicek, I live in the Pontifical Polish College, and I'm studying moral theology. Holy Father, regarding the priestly ministry at the service of our people, after the example of Christ and his mission, how would you advise us to remain available and happy in the service of God's people? What human qualities do you suggest and recommend that we cultivate in order to be images of the Good Shepherd and to live what you have called "the mysticism of encounter"?

I have spoken principally about things that one must do in prayer. However, I'll pick up on the last thing you said, to add something to all that I've said and that has been said and that may lead right to your question. You said: "The mysticism of encounter." Encounter. The capacity for encounter. The ability to hear, to listen to other people. The ability to seek together the way, the method, so many things. This encounter. And it also means not being frightened, not being frightened of things. The good shepherd must not be frightened. Maybe he feels fear inside, but he is never really scared. He knows that the Lord comes to his aid. Encounter the people entrusted to your care as a pastor; encounter your Bishop. The encounter with your Bishop is important. It is also important that the Bishop allow himself to be met. It's important . . . because, yes, sometimes one hears: "Have you told this to your Bishop?" "Yes, I requested an audience, and I requested an audience four months ago. I am still waiting!" This is not good. Go to the Bishop and may the Bishop allow himself to be found. Dialogue, and I would especially like to speak of one thing: the encounter among priests, among yourselves. Priestly friendship: this is a treasure, a treasure that we must cultivate among ourselves—friendship among you, priestly friendship. Not everyone can be close friends. But how beautiful a priestly friendship is! When priests, like two brothers, three brothers, four brothers, know one another, talk about their problems, their joys, their expectations, many things . . . priestly friendship. Seek this, it is important. Be friends. I think this helps a great deal in living the priestly life, the spiritual life, the apostolic life, community life and also the intellectual life: priestly friendship. If I were to meet a priest who said to me: "I have never had a friend," I would think that this priest has not had one of the most beautiful joys of the priestly life: priestly friendship. This is my hope for you. I hope that you be friends with those whom the Lord places along your path as friends. I wish you this in life. Priestly friendship is a force for perseverance, apostolic joy, courage, and even for humor. It is beautiful, most beautiful! This is what I think.

I thank you for your patience! And now we can pray to Our Lady, asking for her blessing. . . .

A Great Inner Freedom

*Address to the Community of the
Pontifical Ecclesiastical Academy*

Clementine Hall, June 6, 2013

I address to you all my most cordial welcome! . . .

Dear friends, you are training for a particularly demanding ministry in which you will serve directly the Successor of Peter, his charism of unity and communion, and his solicitude for all the Churches. Working in the Papal Representations is moreover a labor which—like every kind of priestly ministry—demands great inner freedom, great inner freedom. Live these years of your training with hard work, generosity and a great heart so that this freedom may really be shaped within you.

But what does having inner freedom mean?

First of all it means being free from personal projects, being free from personal projects. Free from some of the tangible ways in which, perhaps, you may once have conceived of living your priesthood; from the possibility of planning your future; from the prospect of staying for any length of time in a place of "your own" pastoral action. It means, in a certain way, making yourself free also with regard to the culture and mindset from which you come. This is not in order to forget it or even less to deny it, but rather to open yourselves in the charity of understanding different cultures and meeting people who belong to worlds far distant from your own.

Above all it means being alert to ensure you keep free of the ambitions or personal aims that can cause the Church great harm. You must be careful not to make either your own fulfillment or the recognition you might receive both inside and outside the ecclesial community a constant priority. Rather, your priority should be the loftier good of the Gospel cause and the accomplishment of the mission that will be entrusted to you. And I think this being free from ambitions or personal goals is important, it is important. Careerism is a form of leprosy, a leprosy. No careerism, please.

For this reason you must be prepared to integrate all your own views of the Church—however legitimate they may be—and every personal idea or opinion into the horizon of Peter's gaze. You must integrate them into his specific mission at the service of the communion and unity of Christ's flock, of his pastoral charity that embraces the whole world and wishes to be present, partly through the action of the papal representations, especially in those all too often forsaken places where the needs of the Church and of humanity are greater.

In a word, the ministry for which you are preparing yourselves—because you are preparing yourselves for a ministry! Not a profession, a ministry—this ministry asks you to leave yourself, to be detached from yourself. It is possible to achieve this only through an intense spiritual journey and a serious unification of life round the mystery of God's love and the inscrutable plan of his call.

In the light of faith we can experience freedom from our own plans and from our will: not as a cause of frustration or emptying but, rather, as openness to God's superabundant gift that makes our priesthood fertile. Living the ministry at the service of the Successor of Peter and of the Churches to which you will be sent might seem demanding, but it will enable you, so to speak, to be and to breathe in the heart of the Church and of her catholicity. Moreover this is a special gift since, as Pope Benedict XVI himself reminded your community, "wherever there is openness to the objectivity of catholicity, there is also the principle of authentic personalization" (*Address to the Pontifical Ecclesiastical Academy*, June 10, 2011).

Take great care of your spiritual life which is the source of inner freedom. Without prayer inner freedom does not exist. You will be able to treasure the means of conformation to Christ that is proper to priestly spirituality by cultivating the life of prayer and by making your daily work the training-ground for your sanctification. I am pleased to recall here the figure of Bl. John XXIII, the anniversary of whose death we celebrated a few days ago. His service as papal representative was one of the areas—and by no means the least significant—in which his holiness was formed. In rereading his writings, his constant painstaking care of his soul in the midst of the most varied occupations in the ecclesial and political areas is striking. This gave rise to his interior freedom, the exterior joy he communicated and the effectiveness of his pastoral and diplomatic action.

So it was that he noted in his *Journal of a Soul* during the Spiritual Exercises of 1948: "The older I become, the more experience I gain, the better I recognize that the most reliable way to my personal sanctification and the best outcome of my service to the Holy See remains the vigilant effort to reduce everything, principles, addresses, positions, business, to the greatest possible simplicity and calmness; with attention always to prune from my vine all that is only useless foliage . . . and to go straight to what is truth, justice, charity, especially charity. Every other system of behaving is solely posturing and the search for personal affirmation which is soon betrayed and becomes cumbersome and ridiculous" (*Edizioni di San Paolo: Cinisello Balsamo 2000*, p. 497). He wanted to prune his vine, to be rid of the foliage, to prune it.

A few years later, after concluding his long service as a papal representative and being appointed Patriarch of Venice, he wrote: "I now find myself in the midst of the ministry for souls. Actually I have always held that for clerics the so-called 'diplomacy!' must always be imbued with a pastoral spirit; otherwise it counts for nothing, and makes a holy mission ridiculous" (*ibid.*, pp. 513-514).

This is important. Listen well: when in a Nunciature there is a secretary or a nuncio who does not take the path of holiness and lets himself be involved in the many forms and manners of spiritual worldliness, he makes himself ridiculous and everyone laughs at him. Please do not make yourselves a laughing stock, be holy or return to your diocese to be a parish priest; but do not be ridiculous in diplomatic life, where there are so many perils in the spiritual life of a priest.

I would like also to say a word to the Sisters—thank you!—who carry out their daily service in a religious and Franciscan spirit. They are the good Mothers who accompany you with their prayers, with their simple and essential words and especially with the example of their faithfulness, devotion and love. With them I would like to thank the lay staff who work in the house. Theirs is a hidden but important presence that enables you to live your time in the Academy with tranquility and hard work.

Dear priests, I hope you will undertake your service to the Holy See in the same spirit as that of Blessed John XXIII. I ask you to pray for me and I entrust you to the care of the Virgin Mary and of St. Anthony Abbot, your patron. May you be accompanied by the assurance of my remembrance and my blessing, which I warmly extend to all your loved ones. Many thanks.

Conform Yourselves Always More to Him

Address to the Plenary of the Congregation for the Clergy

Clementine Hall, October 3, 2014

I address to each of you a warm greeting and my sincere thanks for sharing the Holy See's concern for ordained ministers and their pastoral work. I thank Cardinal Beniamino Stella for the words with which he introduced this meeting. What I would like to tell you concerns three subjects, which correspond to the goals and activity of this Dicastery: vocation, formation, evangelization.

Returning to the image in the Gospel of Matthew, I like comparing the vocation to the ordained ministry to the "treasure hidden in a field" (13:44). It is truly a treasure that God places from the beginning in the hearts of some men; those whom He has chosen and called to follow him in this special state of life. This treasure, which needs to be discovered and brought to light, is not meant to "enrich" just someone. The one called to the ministry is not the "master" of his vocation, but the administrator of a gift that God has entrusted to him for the good of all people, rather, of all men and women, including those who have distanced themselves from religious practice or do not profess faith in Christ. At the same time, the whole of the Christian community is the guardian of the treasure of these vocations, destined for his service, and it must be ever more conscious of the duty to promote them, welcome them and accompany them with affection.

God never ceases to call some to follow and serve Him in the ordained ministry. We too, however, must do our part, through formation, which is the response of man, of the Church to God's gift, that gift that God gives through vocations. It means guarding and fostering vocations, that they may bear ripe fruit. They are "diamonds in the rough" ready to be carefully polished with respect for the conscience of the candidates and with patience, so that they may shine among the People of God. Formation is therefore not a unilateral act by which someone transmits theological or spiritual notions. Jesus did not say to those he called: "Come, let me explain," "Follow me, I will teach you": no! The formation offered by Christ to his disciples came rather as a "come, and follow me," "do as I do," and this is the method that today too, the Church wants to adopt for her ministers. The formation of which we speak is a discipular experience which draws one to Christ and conforms one ever more to Him.

Precisely for this reason, it cannot be a limited task, because priests never stop being disciples of Jesus, who follow Him. Sometimes we proceed with celerity, at other times our step is hesitant, we stop and we may even fall, but always staying on the path. Therefore, formation understood as discipleship accompanies the ordained minister his entire life and regards his person as a whole, intellectually, humanly and spiritually. Initial and ongoing formation are distinct because each requires different methods and timing, but they are two halves of one reality, the life of a disciple cleric, in love with his Lord and steadfastly following him.

Such path of discovery and evaluation of a vocation has a precise purpose: evangelization. Every vocation is missionary and the mission of ordained ministers is evangelization, in all its forms. It starts in the first place with "being," in order to then be translated into "doing." Priests are united in a sacramental brotherhood, therefore, the first form of evangelization is the witness of brotherhood and of communion among themselves and with their bishop. From such a communion can arise a powerful missionary zeal—which frees ordained ministers from the comfortable temptation of being over-anxious about the opinion of others and of their own well-being, than inspired by pastoral love—in order to proclaim the Gospel, to the remotest peripheries.

In this mission of evangelization, priests are called to grow in the awareness of being pastors, sent to stand in the midst of their flock, to render the Lord present through the Eucharist and to dispense his mercy. This is what it means to "be" priests, it is not just limited to what priests "do"; they are free from all spiritual worldliness, conscious that their life is first and foremost about evangelizing even before their work.

How beautiful it is to see priests joyous in their vocation, with a deep serenity, that sustains them even in moments of fatigue and pain! And this never comes about without prayer, prayer from the heart, from that dialogue with the Lord . . . who is the heart, so to speak, of priestly life. We need priests, there is a lack of vocations. The Lord calls, but it is not enough. And we bishops are tempted to take the young men who present themselves without discernment. This is bad for the Church!

Please, one must carefully study the evolution of a vocation! See whether it comes from the Lord, whether the man is healthy, whether the man is well-balanced, whether the man is capable of giving life, of evangelizing, whether the man is capable of forming a family and renouncing this in order to follow Jesus. Today we have so many problems, and in many dioceses, because some bishops made the mistake of taking those who at times have been expelled from other seminaries or religious houses because they need priests. Please! We must consider the good of the People of God.

Dear brothers and sisters, the themes that you have been discussing in these days of Assembly are of great importance. A vocation cared for by means of ongoing formation, in communion, will become a powerful instrument of evangelization, at the service of the People of God. May the Lord enlighten you in your reflections, may my blessing also go with you. And please, I ask you to pray for me and for my service to the Church. Thank you.

Remember Where You Were Taken From

Address on the Fiftieth Anniversary of the Conciliar Decrees
Optatam Totius *and* Presbyterorum Ordinis

Regia Hall, November 20, 2015

A priest's path to holiness begins in the seminary!

Since the vocation to the priesthood is a gift that God gives to some for the good of all, I would like to share some thoughts with you, starting with the relationship between priests and others, according to number 3 of *Presbyterorum Ordinis*, which is like a small compendium of the theology of the priesthood, taken from the Letter to the Hebrews: "Priests, who are taken from among men and ordained for men in the things that belong to God in order to offer gifts and sacrifices for sins, nevertheless live on earth with other men as brothers."

Let us consider these three circumstances: "*taken from among men,*" "*ordained for men,*" and present "*on earth with other men.*"

The priest is a man who is born *into a certain human context*; there he learns the primary values, absorbs the spirituality of the people and acclimates to the relationships. Priests too have a history; they are not "mushrooms" that suddenly spring in a Cathedral on the day of their ordination. It is important that formators and the priests themselves remember this and are able to take account of this personal history along the path of formation. On ordination day I always tell the priests, the new priests: remember where you were taken from, from the flock, never forget your mother and your grandmother! This is what Paul said to Timothy, and I say it again today. This means that you cannot become a priest believing that one has been formed in a laboratory, no; it begins in the family with the "tradition" of the Faith and with the whole family experience. It must be personalized, because it is a concrete person that is called to discipleship and the priesthood, taking into account that in each case Christ is the Master to follow and after whom to model oneself.

In this regard I like to recall that fundamental "center of pastoral vocation" which is the family, the domestic Church and the first and most fundamental place of human formation, where the desire for a life conceived as a vocational path can burgeon in young people, to be followed with commitment and generosity.

In families and all the other community contexts—school, parishes, associations, groups of friends—we learn to have relationships with real people, we are molded by our relationships with them, and we also become who we are because of them.

A good priest, therefore, is first of all a man with his own humanity, who knows his own history, with its riches and its wounds, and who has learned to make peace with it, reaching an underlying serenity, that of a disciple of the Lord. Human formation is therefore a necessity for priests so that they learn not to be dominated by their limitations, but instead to build on their talents.

A priest who is a peaceful man will know how to spread serenity around him, even in the most trying of moments, conveying the beauty of his relationship with the Lord. It is not normal for a priest to be often sad, nervous or harsh of character; it is not okay and it does no good, neither for the priest, nor for his people. If you have an illness, if you're overwrought, go to the doctor! Go to the spiritual doctor and the medical doctor: both of them will give you medicine that will be good for you! The faithful should not have to pay for the neurosis of the priests! Do not lambast the faithful; be close at heart to them.

We priests are apostles of joy, we proclaim the Gospel, that is, the "good news" par excellence; it is certainly not we who give strength to the Gospel—some believe that—but we can either help or hinder the encounter between the Gospel and people. Our humanity is the "earthen vessel" in which we safeguard the treasure of God, a vessel which we must take care of, in order to properly pass on its precious content.

A priest cannot lose his roots; he always remains a man of the people and of the culture that engendered him. Our roots help us to remember who we are and where Christ has called us. We priests do not drop from above, but instead we are called, called by God, who takes us "from among men," so as to be "*for men*." Allow me to share an anecdote. In the diocese, years ago . . . no, not in the diocese, it was in the Society, there was a very good priest, he was young, and had been a priest for two years. He became confused, and spoke with his spiritual director, with his superiors and with the doctors, saying: "I'm leaving, I can't any more, I am leaving." After thinking things over—I knew his mother, they were humble people—I said to him: "Why don't you go to your mom and talk with her about this?" He went and he spent the whole day with his mother, and he came back changed. His mother gave him two spiritual "slaps," she told him three or four things, put him in his place, and he went on. Why? Because he went to the root. This is why it is important to never remove the roots of where we come from. In the seminary you have to do mental prayer. . . . Yes, of course, this must be done, to learn. . . . But before all else you pray the way your mom taught you, and then you move forward. The root is always there, the root of family, as you learned to pray as a child, even with the same words, begin to pray like that. Then you will go forward in prayer.

Here is the second step: "*ordained for men.*"

Here is a key point to the life and ministry of priests. Answering God's call, you become a priest *to serve your brothers and sisters.* The images of Christ that we take as a reference for the ministry of priests are clear: He is the "High Priest," close in the same way to God and to mankind; he is the "Servant," who washes feet and who becomes a neighbor to the weakest; he is the "Good Shepherd," who always has as his goal the care of the flock.

There are three images that we should look to when thinking about the ministry of priests: sent to serve men, to help them obtain the mercy of God, and to proclaim his Word of life. We are not priests for ourselves, and our sanctification is closely linked to that of our people, our unction for their unction; you are anointed for your people. Knowing and remembering that he is "ordained for men"—the holy people, the People of God—helps a priest not to think of himself, to be authoritative and not authoritarian, firm but not harsh, joyful but not superficial, in short, to be a pastor and not an official. Today, in both Readings of the Mass, we clearly see the people's ability to rejoice, when the temple is restored and purified, while at the same time we see the chief priests and scribes' incapacity for joy at seeing Jesus drive the merchants out of the temple. A priest must learn to rejoice, moreover he must never lose the capacity for joy: if he loses it something is not right. I tell you honestly, I'm afraid of rigidity, I am afraid. Rigid priests . . . stay away!

130

They bite you! And I recall an expression of St. Ambrose, from the fourth century: "Where there is mercy there is the spirit of the Lord, and where there is rigidity there are only his ministers." A minister without the Lord becomes rigid, and this is a danger to God's people. Be pastors, not officials.

The People of God and all of humanity are the beneficiaries of the mission of priests, and all the work of formation is geared toward this mission. Human, intellectual and spiritual formation flow naturally into this ministry, which such formation provides with tools, virtues and personal predisposition. When all of this harmonizes and blends with true missionary zeal, along the path of an entire lifetime, the priest can fulfill the mission that Christ has entrusted to his Church.

Furthermore, what is born of the people must remain with the people; the priest is always "*on earth with other men,*" he is not a professional in pastoral ministry or in evangelization, who arrives and does what he must—perhaps well, but as if it were a trade—and then leaves to live a separate life. One becomes a priest to be on earth with the people: closeness. And if I may, brother bishops, we bishops should also have this closeness with our priests. This also applies to us! How often do we hear priests complain: "Well, I called the bishop because I have a problem. . . . The secretary, the secretary told me he is very busy, that he is out, that he will not be able to see me for another three months. . . ." Two things. The first: a bishop is always busy, thanks be to God, but if you bishops receive a call from a priest and cannot receive him because you have a lot of work, at least pick up the phone, call him and ask: "Is it urgent? Is it not urgent? When, come that day . . . ," in this way you are close. There are bishops who seem to move away from the priests. . . . Closeness, at least a phone call! That is fatherly love, fraternity. And the other thing: "No, I have a conference in the city and then I have to make a trip to America, and then . . ." But, listen, the decree of Trent concerning residence is still in force! And if you do not feel like staying in the diocese, resign and travel the world doing a different, very good apostolate. However, if you're the bishop of that diocese: residence. These two things: closeness and residence. This is for us bishops! One becomes a priest to be on earth with the people.

The good that the priests can do is born mainly from their closeness and their tender love for people. They are neither philanthropists nor officials; priests are fathers and brothers. The fatherhood of a priest does so much good.

Closeness, the depths of mercy, a loving gaze: to experience the beauty of a life lived according to the Gospel and the love of God, which is also made concrete through his ministers. God never refuses. And here I think of the confessional. You can always find ways of giving absolution; to welcome the good. But sometimes you cannot absolve. There are priests who say: "No, because of this I cannot absolve you, go away." This is not the way. If you cannot give absolution, explain and say: "God loves you so much, God loves you. There are so many ways to reach God. I cannot give you absolution; I give you the blessing. But come back, always come back here, and whenever you come back I'll give you a blessing as a sign that God loves you." And that man or woman will go away full of joy because he found the image of the Father, who never refuses; in one way or another, he has embraced that person.

This too is a good examination of conscience for a priest: If the Lord were to return today, where would he find me? "For where your treasure is, there will your heart be also" (Mt 6:21). And where is my heart? Is it among the people, praying with and for the people, involved with their joys and sufferings, or is it rather among worldly things, earthly affairs, in my private "spaces"? A priest cannot have a private space, because he is always either with the Lord or with the people. I think of those priests that I knew in my city, when there were no answering machines, who slept with a phone on the bedside table. At whatever time people would call, they got up to give the anointing: no one died without the sacraments! They did not even have a private space when they rested. That is apostolic zeal. The answer to the question, "Where is my heart?" can help every priest to guide his life and his ministry toward the Lord.

The Council left the Church "precious pearls." Like the merchant in the Gospel of Matthew (13:45), today we go in search of them, to bring new impetus and new instruments for the mission that the Lord has entrusted to us.

One thing that I would like to add to the text—sorry!—is vocational discernment, the admission to seminary. Seek the health of that young man, the spiritual, physical, material, physical and mental health. Once, when I had just been appointed master of novices in 1972, I took the results of a personality test to the psychologist, it was a simple test that was done as one of the elements of discernment. She was a good woman, and also a good doctor. She said to me: "This one has this problem, but he can proceed if he does so in this way. . . ." She was also a good Christian, but in some cases was adamant: "This one cannot"—"But doctor, this young man is so good"—"He is good now, but know that there are young people who unconsciously know, they are not aware of it, but unconsciously they feel that they are mentally ill, and seek strong structures that will protect them in life, in order to go on. And they go on fine, until the moment comes when they feel well established and there the problems begin"—"It seems a bit strange to me. . . ." And I will never forget her response, it was like that of the Lord to Ezekiel: "Father, have you ever wondered why there are so many police officers who torture? They enter young, they seem healthy but when they feel confident the illness begins to emerge. Those are the strong institutions that these unconsciously sick ones seek: the police, the army, the clergy. . . . And we all know that there are many illnesses which come out." It's curious. When I realize that a young man is too rigid, too fundamental- ist, I do not have confidence; in the background there is something that he himself does not know. But when they feel confident . . . Ezekiel 16, I cannot remember the verse, but it is when the Lord tells his people all that he did for them: he found them when they were just born, and he clothed them, he espoused them. . . . "And then, when you felt secure, you prostituted yourself." It is a rule, a rule of life. Eyes open to the mis- sion in seminaries. Eyes open.

A Mother Church

To Participants in the Ecclesial Convention of the Diocese of Rome

Paul VI Hall, June 16, 2014

Cardinal Vallini spoke about this path of pastoral and missionary conversion. It is a path that one takes and one must take and we still have the grace to be able to take it. Conversion is not easy, because it means changing one's life, changing one's ways, changing so many things, even changing the soul. But this path of conversion will give us the identity of a people who knows how to bear children, not a sterile people! If we, as the Church, do not know how to bear children, something is not working! The great challenge for the Church today is to become mother: mother! Not a perfectly organized nonprofit, with so many pastoral plans. . . . We need them, sure. . . . But that is not essential, it is just a help. A help to what? To the motherhood of the Church. If the Church is not mother, it is sad to say that she becomes a spinster, but she does become a spinster! That's how it is: she bears no fruit. The Church not only makes children, but it is part of her identity to make children, that is, to evangelize, as Paul VI says in *Evangelii Nuntiandi*. The Church's identity is this: to evangelize, that is, to make children. I think of our mother Sarah, who grew old without children; I think of Elizabeth, the wife of Zechariah, old without children; I think of Naomi, another old woman without descendants. . . . And these barren women did bear children, they were given descendants: the Lord is capable of doing that! That is why the Church must do something, must change, must convert in order to become mother. She must be fruitful! Fruitfulness is a grace that we today need to ask from the Holy Spirit, so that we can go forward in our pastoral and missionary conversion. This is not a question of seeking to proselytize, no, no! To go ring the bell: "Would you like to come to this association called the Catholic Church? . . ." We need to make a card, another member. . . . The Church—Benedict XVI told us—does not grow through proselytism, she grows through attraction, maternal attraction, offering her motherhood: she grows through ten-derness, her maternity, the witness that generates ever more and more children. She is a little aged, our Mother Church. . . . We shouldn't call her "Grandma Church," but still she is a little older. . . . We must reju-venate her! We must rejuvenate her, but not by taking her to the plastic surgeon, no! This is not the true rejuvenation of the Church, it doesn't work. The Church grows younger when she is capable of generating more children; she grows younger the more she becomes mother. This is our mother, the Church and our love for children. To be in the Church is to be at home, with mom; at mom's house. This is the gran-deur of revelation. . . .

I have only one word to say: welcome. This is it, welcome. And another that you said: tenderness. A mother is tender, she knows how to caress. But when we see the poor people who go to the parish, and they don't know how to move in this setting, because they don't often go to the parish, and they find a secretary who yells, who closes the door: "No, for you to do this, you have to pay this, this and this much! And you have to do this and this. . . . Take this form and you have to. . . ." These people don't feel like they are at their mother's house! They might feel like they are at the secretary's office but not at their mother's house. And these secretaries, the new "ostiaries" of the Church! Being parish secre-tary means opening the front door of the mother's home, not closing it! And one can close the door in many ways. In Buenos Aires there was a famous parish secretary: they called her the "tarantula" . . . I'll say no more! To know how to open the door in the moment: welcome and tenderness.

Priests, pastors and assistant pastors also have so much work to do and I understand that at times they are a little tired; but a parish priest who is too impatient does no good! Sometimes I understand, I under-stand. . . . Once I had to listen to a humble woman, very humble, who had left the Church when she was young; now she was the mother of a family, she came back to the Church and said: "Father, I left the Church because in the parish, as a little girl"—I don't know if she was in confir-mation class, I am not sure—"a woman with a baby came and asked the pastor to perform the Baptism. . . ."—this was a long time ago and not here in Rome, in another place—"and the parish priest said yes, but she would have to pay. . . . 'But I have no money!' 'Go home, take whatever you have, bring it to me and I will baptize the child.'" And that woman was speaking to me in the presence of God! This happens. . . . This does not signify welcome, this is closing the door! In the present: tenderness and welcome. . . .

When they come to the parish . . . what attitude should we take? We must always welcome everyone with a big heart, as in a family, asking the Lord to make us capable of participating in the difficulties and the problems that often children and young people encounter in their lives.

We must have the heart of Jesus, who "when he saw the crowds, he had compassion for them, because they were harassed and helpless, like sheep without a shepherd" (Mt 9:36). Seeing the crowds, he feels compassion for them. I like to dream of a Church who lives the compassion of Jesus. Compassion is to "suffer with," to feel what the others feel, to accompany them emotionally. It is Mother Church, who caresses her children with compassion like a mother. A Church that has a heart without borders, and not only the heart: also the gaze, the sweetness of Jesus' gaze, which is often much more eloquent than so many words. People expect to find in us the gaze of Jesus, sometimes without even knowing it, that serene gaze, a happiness that seeps into the heart. But— as your representatives said—it takes a whole parish to be a welcoming community, not just the priests and catechists. The whole parish! Welcome. . . .

We must rethink how welcoming our parishes are: whether the hours of activities encourage the participation of young people; whether we are capable of speaking their language, of reaching out by other means (as for example sports, new technologies) for opportunities to proclaim the Gospel. Let us become bold in exploring new ways with which our communities can be homes where the door is always open. An open door! And it is important that the welcome is followed by a clear proposal of the faith; many times a proposal of the faith may not be explicit, but is conveyed by attitude, by witness: in this institution called the Church, in this institution called the parish one breathes the air of faith, because one believes in the Lord Jesus.

I will ask you to study carefully these things that I have said: this orphanhood, and to study how to recover the memory of the family; how to bring warmth and gratuitousness to the parish, so that it won't be an institution tied solely to the conditions of the moment. No, let it have a history, let it be on a journey of pastoral conversion. Let it know how to welcome with tenderness in the present, and how to send forth her children with hope and patience.

I truly appreciate priests, because being a pastor is not easy. It's easier to be a bishop than a pastor! Because we bishops always have the option of stepping back, or hiding behind "His Excellency," and that is our defense! But to be a pastor, when they knock on your door: "Father this, here father, there father. . . ." It's not easy! When someone comes to you to speak about family problems, or about a deceased person, or when the so-called "charity girls" come to gossip about the so-called "catechesis girls." . . . It's not easy being a pastor!

Pastor Servants of God and Fathers of the People

*Address to the Community of the
Pontifical Lombard Seminary*

Clementine Hall, January 25, 2016

Dear Brothers and Sisters,

I greet you affectionately and I thank Cardinal Scola for his courteous words. I am happy to meet with you on the occasion of the fiftieth anniversary of this institution: so, you also celebrate in the Holy Year of Mercy a Jubilee of Thanksgiving to God, rock on which life is founded, because "His faithfulness endures for ever" (Cf. Ps 117:2). Do not forget this: God is faithful.

Bl. Paul VI blessed the Lombard Seminary on November 11, 1965, so that this house would be inhabited at the end of Vatican Council II, in which the Fathers perceived strongly that "the walls having been pulled down, which for too much time had shut the Church in a privileged citadel, the time had arrived to proclaim the Gospel in a new way" (*Misericordiae Vultus*, no. 4). Thus, in the "Roman years," which are not only of study, but of true and proper priestly formation, you also are preparing yourselves to follow the impulse of the Spirit, to be the "future of the Church" according to God's heart; not according to the preferences of each one or the fashions of the moment, but as the proclamation of the Gospel requires. To prepare oneself well one must work in depth, but above all one must undergo an interior conversion, which daily roots the ministry in Jesus' first call, and revives it in a personal relation with Him, as the Apostle Paul did, whose conversion, in fact, we recall today.

In this connection, I would like to draw your attention to a model you already know well: St. Charles Borromeo. Fr. de Certeau has presented his life as a constant "movement of conversion," tending to reflect the image of the Pastor: "He identified himself with this image, nourished it with his life, knowing that the discourse passes in reality through the price of blood: *sanguinis ministri*, were the true priests for him. Therefore, he realized the image by losing himself. He put all his 'passion' into reproducing it" (*Dizionario Biografico degli Italiani*, XX, 1977, p. 263). Thus, holy Pastors, such as Borromeo, carried out the great work of the time, which culminated in the holding of the Council of Trent. Dear friends, you are heirs and witnesses of a great history of sanctity, which sinks its roots in your patrons, the Bishops Ambrose and Charles, and in most recent times has had among its pupils, three Blesseds and three Servants of God. This is the goal to which you should strive!

However, a temptation appears on the way that must be rejected: that of "*normality*," of a Pastor for whom a "normal" life is enough. Thus this priest begins to be contented with some attention received, he judges the ministry on the basis of his successes and he abandons himself to research of what pleases him, becoming tepid and without a real interest in others. Instead, for us "normality" is pastoral holiness, the gift of life. If a priest chooses to be only a normal person, he will be a mediocre priest or worse.

St. Charles wanted Pastors that were servants of God and fathers of the people, especially of the poor. But—it always does us good to remember this—he can only proclaim the words of life who makes of his own life a constant dialogue with the Word of God, or, better, with God who speaks to us. Entrusted to you during these years is the mission to train yourselves in this dialogue of life: knowledge of the various disciplines that you study is not an end in itself, but is *concretized* in the colloquy of prayer and in a real encounter with persons. It does no good to be formed "in watertight compartments"; prayer, education and pastoral care are bearer stones of one building: they must always be solidly united to support one another, well cemented between them, so that the priests of today and tomorrow are *spiritual men and merciful pastors*, interiorly unified by the love of the Lord and able to spread the joy of the Gospel in the simplicity of life. In fact, evangelization, today, seems called to follow again the way of simplicity. Simplicity of life, which avoids every form of duplicity and worldliness, to which genuine communion with the Lord and with brothers suffices; simplicity of language: not preachers of complex doctrines, but heralds of Christ, dead and risen for us.

Another essential aspect that I would like to stress, to be a good priest, is the necessity of contact and *closeness with the Bishop*. The characteristic of the diocesan priest is in fact the diocese itself, and the diocese itself is his cornerstone in his frequent relation with the Bishop, in dialogue and discernment with him. A priest who does not have an assiduous relation with his Bishop isolates himself slowly from the diocesan body and his fruitfulness diminishes, precisely because he does not engage in dialogue with the Father of the Diocese.

Finally, I would like to tell you that I rejoice not only because of your profitable commitment in your studies, but also because of the international dimension of your community: you come from various regions of Italy, of Africa, of Latin America, of Asia and of other European countries. I hope you will cultivate the beauty of friendship and the art of establishing relations, to create a priestly fraternity that is stronger than the particular differences. Thus you will always render this house welcoming and enriching! Henceforth, when I go to the Basilica of St. Mary Major, I will think of this meeting and I will remember you before the Virgin Mother. But you also, I recommend, do the same for me! Thank you.

Meetings with Bishops

Ministers Capable of Warming People's Hearts

Apostolic Journey to Rio de Janeiro on the Occasion of the Twenty-Eight World Youth Day

Address to the Bishops of Brazil

Archbishop's House, Rio de Janeiro, July 27, 2013

Dear brothers, unless we train ministers capable of warming people's hearts, of walking with them in the night, of dialoguing with their hopes and disappointments, of mending their brokenness, what hope can we have for our present and future journey? It isn't true that God's presence has been dimmed in them. Let us learn to look at things more deeply. What is missing is someone to warm their heart, as was the case with the disciples of Emmaus (cf. Lk 24:32).

That is why it is important to devise and ensure a suitable formation, one which will provide persons able to step into the night without being overcome by the darkness and losing their bearings; able to listen to people's dreams without being seduced and to share their disappointments without losing hope and becoming bitter; able to sympathize with the brokenness of others without losing their own strength and identity.

What is needed is a solid human, cultural, effective, spiritual and doctrinal formation. . . . It is not enough that formation be considered a vague priority, either in documents or at meetings. What is needed is the practical wisdom to set up lasting educational structures on the local, regional and national levels and to take them to heart as Bishops, without sparing energy, concern and personal interest. The present situation calls for quality formation at every level. Bishops may not delegate this task. You cannot delegate this task, but must embrace it as something fundamental for the journey of your Churches.

A Change of Attitudes

*Apostolic Journey to Rio de Janeiro on the
Occasion of the Twenty-Eighth World Youth Day*

*Address to the Leadership of the
Episcopal Conferences of Latin America*

Sumaré Study Center, Rio de Janeiro, July 28, 2013

Aparecida considered Pastoral Conversion to be a necessity. This conversion involves believing in the Good News, believing in Jesus Christ as the bearer of God's Kingdom as it breaks into the world and in his victorious presence over evil, believing in the help and guidance of the Holy Spirit, believing in the Church, the Body of Christ and the prolonging of the dynamism of the incarnation.

Consequently, we, as pastors, need to ask questions about the actual state of the Churches which we lead. These questions can serve as a guide in examining where the dioceses stand in taking up the spirit of Aparecida; they are questions which we need to keep asking as an examination of conscience.

1. Do we see to it that our work, and that of our priests, is more pastoral than administrative? Who primarily benefits from our efforts, the Church as an organization or the People of God as a whole?

2. Do we fight the temptation simply to react to complex problems as they arise? Are we creating a proactive mindset? Do we promote opportunities and possibilities to manifest God's mercy? Are we conscious of our responsibility for refocusing pastoral approaches and the functioning of Church structures for the benefit of the faithful and society?

3. In practice, do we make the lay faithful sharers in the Mission? Do we offer them the word of God and the sacraments with a clear awareness and conviction that the Holy Spirit makes himself manifest in them?

4. Is pastoral discernment a habitual criterion, through the use of Diocesan Councils? Do such Councils and Parish Councils, whether pastoral or financial, provide real opportunities for lay people to participate in pastoral consultation, organization and planning? The good functioning of these Councils is critical. I believe that on this score, we are far behind.

5. As pastors, bishops and priests, are we conscious and convinced of the mission of the lay faithful and do we give them the freedom to continue discerning, in a way befitting their growth as disciples, the mission which the Lord has entrusted to them? Do we support them and accompany them, overcoming the temptation to manipulate them or infantilize them? Are we constantly open to letting ourselves be challenged in our efforts to advance the good of the Church and her mission in the world?

6. Do pastoral agents and the faithful in general feel part of the Church, do they identify with her and bring her closer to the baptized who are distant and alienated?

As can be appreciated, what is at stake here are *attitudes*. Pastoral Conversion is chiefly concerned with attitudes and reforming our lives. A change of attitudes is necessarily something ongoing: "it is a process," and it can only be kept on track with the help of guidance and discernment. It is important always to keep in mind that the compass preventing us from going astray is that of Catholic identity, understood as membership in the Church.

Know the Parish Inside Out

Letter to the President of the Bishops' Conference of Argentina on the Occasion of the Beatification of Fr. José Gabriele Brochero

From the Vatican, September 14, 2013

Today I like to imagine Brochero the parish priest on the back of his mule with the white mane (*malacara*), crossing the broad, dry and desolate roads of his 200-square-kilometer parish. He would go from house to house, seeking out your great-grandparents and your great-great-grandparents to ask them whether they needed anything and invite them to do the spiritual exercises of St. Ignatius of Loyola. He knew his parish inside out. He did not stay in the sacristy combing the sheep.

The visit of Brochero the Gaucho Priest brought Jesus himself to every family. He would take with him an image of Our Lady, a prayer book with the word of God and his kit to celebrate daily Mass. They would invite him in to drink *mate*; they would chat and Brochero would speak to them in a way they could all understand so that the faith and love he himself felt for Jesus would well up in their hearts.

José Gabriel Brochero centered his pastoral action on prayer. He had barely arrived in his parish when he began to take men and women to Córdoba to do spiritual exercises with the Jesuit fathers. With great sacrifice they first crossed the Sierras Grandes, covered with snow in winter, to pray in the region's capital Córdoba! Afterward, they worked hard to build the Holy House for the exercises in the parish! They prayed at length there before the crucifix in order to know, feel and enjoy the immense love of Jesus' heart, and it all ended with God's pardon in confession, with a priest who was full of love and mercy—immense mercy!

His apostolic courage, his missionary zeal, the bravery in his heart, compassionate like the heart of Jesus—that made him say: "There'll be trouble if the devil robs me of a single soul!"—spurred Brochero to win over crooks and difficult fellow countrymen to God. One can count by the thousands the men and women who, thanks to Brochero's priestly

146

ministry, gave up their vices and quarrels. They received the sacraments during the spiritual exercises and with them the power and light of faith to be good sons and daughters of God, good brothers and sisters and good parents in a great community of friends committed to the good of all and who respected and helped each other.

A contemporary pastoral approach is very important in a beatification. Brochero the Gaucho Priest had a currently relevant approach to the Gospel. He was a pioneer in going out to the geographical and existential peripheries to take God's love and mercy to everyone. He did not stay in the parish office, he tired himself out riding his mule and in the end fell ill with leprosy as a result of going out to find people as a *callejero*, a "street priest" of faith. This is what Jesus wants today, missionary disciples, street priests of faith!

Brochero was an ordinary man, frail like the rest of us, but he knew the love of Jesus, his heart was forged by God's mercy. He was able to come out from the cavern of "I-me-my-with me-for me," of the small-minded selfishness from which we all suffer, he conquered himself, with God's help, he overcame those inner forces that the devil uses to chain us to comfort, to the search for fleeting pleasure, to the lack of incentive to work. Brochero listened to God's call. He chose the sacrifice of working for his Kingdom, for the common good that the great dignity of every person as a child of God deserves. He was faithful to the end: he continued praying and celebrating Mass even when he was blind and ill with leprosy.

Today let us permit Brochero the Gaucho Priest, with his mule and all, to enter the house of our heart and invite us to prayer, to the encounter with Jesus that sets us free from attachments so that we may go out to the street and seek our brother or sister, to touch the flesh of Christ in those who suffer, who need God's love. Only in this way shall we savor the joy that Brochero the Gaucho Priest felt, a foretaste of the happiness he now enjoys as a blessed in heaven.

Love and Priests

Letter to Participants in the Extraordinary General Assembly of the Italian Episcopal Conference, Assisi, November 10-13, 2015

From the Vatican, November 8, 2014

Dear Brothers in the Episcopate,

With these lines I would like to express my closeness to each one of you and to the Churches in the midst of which the Spirit of God has placed you as Pastors. May this same Spirit, with its creative wisdom, give life to the General Assembly that you are beginning, especially dedicated to life and to the permanent formation of the presbyter.

In this regard, your gathering in Assisi leads one immediately to contemplate the great love and veneration that St. Francis fostered for the Hierarchical Holy Mother Church, and in particular for priests, including those whom he recognized as *"pauperculos huius saeculi"* (from *The Testament*).

Among the principal responsibilities that the episcopal ministry entrusts to you is that of confirming, supporting and strengthening these your first collaborators, through whom the motherhood of the Church reaches the entire People of God. How many we have known! How many contributed with their witness to attract us to a consecrated life! How many of them did we learn from and were we molded by! Each one of us gratefully cherishes their names and faces. We saw them expend their lives among the people of our parishes, educating the youth, attentive to families, visiting the sick at home and in hospitals, taking charge of the poor in the awareness that "withdrawing from others to avoid getting soiled is the worst sort of filth" (cf. L. Tolstoy). Free from things and from themselves, they remind all that to lower oneself without holding back is the way for that loftiness that the Gospel calls charity; and that the truest joy is tasted in the fraternity experienced.

Holy priests are forgiven sinners and instruments of forgiveness. Their existence speaks the language of patience and perseverance; they are not spiritual tourists, eternally undecided and dissatisfied, because they know they are in the hands of the One who never fails in His promises and whose Providence is such that nothing can separate them from that belonging. This awareness grows with the pastoral charity with which they surround the people entrusted to them with care and tenderness, until they know them one by one.

Yes, it is still the time for this type of presbyter: "bridges" for the encounter between God and the world, able sentinels who can transmit a richness otherwise lost.

Such priests cannot be improvised: they are forged by the precious formative work of the seminary, and Ordination consecrates them for ever as men of God and servants of His people. It can happen, however, that time cools the generous dedication of the beginning, and it is then of no use to sew new patches onto an old garment: the identity of the presbyter, precisely because it comes from on High, exacts of him a daily journey of re-appropriation, beginning from what made him a minister of Jesus Christ.

The formation of which we speak is an experience of permanent discipleship, which draws one close to Christ and allows one to be ever more conformed to Him. Therefore, it has no end, for priests never stop being disciples of Jesus, they never stop following Him. Thus, formation understood as discipleship sustains the ordained minister his entire life and regards his entire person and his ministry. Initial and ongoing formation are two aspects of one reality: the path of the disciple priest, in love with his Lord and steadfastly following Him (cf. *Address to the Plenary Assembly of the Congregation for the Clergy*, October 3, 2014).

After all, brothers, you know there is no need for clerical priests whose behavior risks distancing people from the Lord, nor for functionary priests who, while playing a role, seek their consolation far from Him. Only one whose gaze is fixed on what is truly essential can renew his "yes" to the gift received and, in life's various seasons, does not cease to make a gift of himself; only one who lets himself be conformed to the Good Shepherd finds unity, peace and strength in the obedience of service; only one who breathes on the horizon of presbyterial fraternity is free from a false conscience, a conscience which presumes to be the epicenter of everything, the only measure of one's feeling and action.

I hope you will have days of listening and discussion, which lead to outlining itineraries of permanent formation, capable of combining the spiritual dimension with the cultural, the community dimension with the pastoral: these are the pillars of life formed according to the Gospel, preserved in daily discipline, in prayer, in controlling the senses, in the care of oneself, in humble and prophetic witness; lives that restore to the Church the trust that she first placed in them.

I accompany you with my prayer and my Blessing, which I extend, through the intercession of the Virgin Mother, to all the priests of the Church in Italy and to those who work in the service of their formation; and I thank you for your prayers for me and for my ministry.

Everyone Is Called, Everyone Is Sent Out

Address to the Bishops of the Episcopal Conference of Austria on Their Ad Limina Visit

Clementine Hall, January 30, 2014

Priests, parish priests should always be mindful that their task of governing is a profoundly spiritual service. It is always the parish priest who must lead the parish community, relying at the same time on the help and the valuable contribution of their various coworkers and on all the lay faithful. We must not run the risk of clouding the sacramental ministry of the priest. In our cities and villages there are brave men and others who are timid, there are Christian missionaries and others who are asleep. And there are many who are searching, even if they do not admit it. Everyone is called, everyone is sent out. However, the place of the call is not necessarily the parish center; the moment is not necessarily a pleasant parish event. The call of God can reach us on the assembly line and in the office, in the supermarket and in the stairwell, i.e., in the places of everyday life.

Close to Your Priests

Meeting with the Bishops of Korea

Sixth Asian Youth Day, August 13-18, 2014

Seoul, August 14, 2014

I ask you to remain ever close to your priests, encouraging them in their daily labors, their pursuit of sanctity and their proclamation of the Gospel of salvation. I ask you to convey to them my affectionate greeting and my gratitude for their dedicated service to God's people. I urge you to remain close to your priests. Close, so that they can see their bishop often. This closeness of the bishop is not only fraternal but also paternal: as they carry out their pastoral ministry, priests often need it. Bishops must not be distant from their priests, or worse, unapproachable. I say this with a heavy heart. Where I come from, some priests would tell me: "I've called the bishop, I've asked to meet him; yet three months have gone by and I have still not received an answer." Brothers, if a priest phones you today and asks to see you, call him back immediately, today or tomorrow. If you don't have time to see him, tell him: "I can't meet you because of this, that and or the other thing, but I wanted to call you and I am here for you." But let them hear their father's response, as quickly as possible. Please, do not be distant from your priests.

The Superficiality That Does Great Harm

Meeting with the Bishops of Asia

Sixth Asian Youth Day, August 13-18, 2014

Shrine of Haemi, August 17, 2014

Superficiality, a tendency to toy with the latest fads, gadgets and distractions, rather than attending to the things that really matter (cf. Phil 1:10). In a culture which glorifies the ephemeral, and offers so many avenues of avoidance and escape, this can present a serious pastoral problem. For the ministers of the Church, it can also make itself felt in an enchantment with pastoral programs and theories, to the detriment of direct, fruitful encounter with our faithful, and others too, especially the young who need solid catechesis and sound spiritual guidance. Without a grounding in Christ, the truths by which we live our lives can gradually recede, the practice of the virtues can become formalistic, and dialogue can be reduced to a form of negotiation or an agreement to disagree. An agreement to disagree . . . so as not to make waves. . . . This sort of superficiality does us great harm.

Offer a Good Formation

*Address to the Bishops of the Episcopal Conference of Chad
on Their Ad Limina Visit*

Clementine Hall, October 2, 2014

Lastly, the fruitfulness and the soundness of evangelization certainly
depend on the preparation of the clergy. . . . Of course, their task is difficult, often carried out in basic, lonely conditions. So as to support them
in their mission, and to ensure that their ministry among the faithful
bears fruit, it is important to offer a good formation in the seminaries. I
know what an investment—of funds and of people—this is for a diocese.
But I highly recommend that you make a concerted effort to choose
and train stable and competent professors. Do not hesitate to commit
yourselves personally, visiting the seminaries yourselves, showing you are
close to the professors and to the seminarians, the better to appreciate
the wealth and understand the short-comings of the syllabus in order to
confirm the former and remedy the latter.

Regarding the permanent formation of the clergy, at the diocesan
level, in order that everyone may participate, it is certainly necessary to
review and remember the needs of the priestly life in all of its aspects—
spiritual, intellectual, moral, pastoral, liturgical—as well as to engender
a sincere and enthusiastic fraternal priesthood.

Vigilance Toward the
Priestly Vocation

*Address to the Bishops of the Episcopal Conference of
Cameroon on Their* Ad Limina *Visit*

Clementine Hall, September 6, 2014

It is also fundamental that the clergy witness to a way of life which professes the Lord, one consistent with the exigencies and principles of the Gospel. I want to express to all the priests my gratitude for the apostolic zeal they show, frequently in difficult and dangerous conditions, and I assure them of my closeness and of my prayer. It is nonetheless important to remain vigilant in the discernment and care of priestly vocations . . . and also to support continuing formation and the spiritual life of priests for whom you must be attentive fathers since the temptations of the world are many, especially those of power, prestige and wealth. On this last point, the counter-witness that might be given by the mismanagement of resources, accrual of personal wealth or wastefulness is particularly scandalous in a region where many people lack the bare necessities of life.

The Essence of the Shepherd

Meeting with the Bishops of the United States

Cathedral of St. Matthew the Apostle,
September 23, 2015

Whenever a hand reaches out to do good or to show the love of Christ, to dry a tear or bring comfort to the lonely, to show the way to one who is lost or to console a broken heart, to help the fallen or to teach those thirsting for truth, to forgive or to offer a new start in God . . . know that the Pope is at your side, the Pope supports you. He puts his hand on your own, a hand wrinkled with age, but by God's grace still able to support and encourage. . . .

We are bishops of the Church, shepherds appointed by God to feed his flock. Our greatest joy is to be shepherds, and only shepherds, pastors with undivided hearts and selfless devotion. We need to preserve this joy and never let ourselves be robbed of it. The evil one roars like a lion, anxious to devour it, wearing us down in our resolve to be all that we are called to be, not for ourselves but in gift and service to the *"Shepherd of our souls"* (1 Pt 2:25).

The heart of our identity is to be sought in constant prayer, in preaching (Acts 6:4) and in shepherding the flock entrusted to our care (Jn 21:15-17; Acts 20:28-31).

Ours must not be just any kind of prayer, but familiar union with Christ, in which we daily encounter his gaze and sense that he is asking us the question: *"Who is my mother? Who are my brothers?"* (Mk 3:31-34). One in which we can calmly reply: *"Lord, here is your mother, here are your brothers! I hand them over to you; they are the ones whom you entrusted to me."* Such trusting union with Christ is what nourishes the life of a pastor.

It is not about preaching complicated doctrines, but joyfully proclaiming Christ who died and rose for our sake. The "style" of our mission should make our hearers feel that the message we preach is meant *"for us."* May the word of God grant meaning and fullness to every aspect of their lives; may the sacraments nourish them with that food which they cannot procure for themselves; may the closeness of the shepherd make them long once again for the Father's embrace. Be vigilant that the flock may always encounter in the heart of their pastor that "taste of eternity" which they seek in vain in the things of this world. May they always hear from you a word of appreciation for their efforts to confirm in liberty and justice the prosperity in which this land abounds. At the same time, may you never lack the serene courage to proclaim that "*we must work not for the food which perishes, but for the food which endures for eternal life*" (Jn 6:27).

Shepherds who do not pasture themselves but are able to step back, away from the center, to "decrease," in order to feed God's family with Christ. Who keep constant watch, standing on the heights to look out with God's eyes on the flock which is his alone. Who ascend to the height of the cross of God's Son, the sole standpoint which opens to the shepherd the heart of his flock.

Shepherds who do not lower our gaze, concerned only with our concerns, but raise it constantly toward the horizons which God opens before us and which surpass all that we ourselves can foresee or plan. Who also watch over ourselves, so as to flee the temptation of narcissism, which blinds the eyes of the shepherd, makes his voice unrecognizable and his actions fruitless. In the countless paths which lie open to your pastoral concern, remember to keep focused on the core which unifies everything: "*You did it unto me*" (Mt 25:31-45).

Certainly it is helpful for a bishop to have the farsightedness of a leader and the shrewdness of an administrator, but we fall into hopeless decline whenever we confuse the power of strength with the strength of that powerlessness with which God has redeemed us. Bishops need to be lucidly aware of the battle between light and darkness being fought in this world. Woe to us, however, if we make of the cross a banner of worldly struggles and fail to realize that the price of lasting victory is allowing ourselves to be wounded and consumed (Phil 2:1-11).

We all know the anguish felt by the first Eleven, huddled together, assailed and overwhelmed by the fear of sheep scattered because the shepherd had been struck. But we also know that we have been given a spirit of courage and not of timidity. So we cannot let ourselves be paralyzed by fear.

I know that you face many challenges, and that the field in which you sow is unyielding and that there is always the temptation to give in to fear, to lick one's wounds, to think back on bygone times and to devise harsh responses to fierce opposition.

And yet we are promoters of the culture of encounter. We are living sacraments of the embrace between God's riches and our poverty. We are witnesses of the abasement and the condescension of God who anticipates in love our every response.

Dialogue is our method, not as a shrewd strategy but out of fidelity to the One who never wearies of visiting the marketplace, even at the eleventh hour, to propose his offer of love (Mt 20:1-16).

The path ahead, then, is dialogue among yourselves, dialogue in your presbyterates, dialogue with lay persons, dialogue with families, dialogue with society. I cannot ever tire of encouraging you to dialogue fearlessly. The richer the heritage which you are called to share with *parrhesia*, the more eloquent should be the humility with which you should offer it. Do not be afraid to set out on that "exodus" which is necessary for all authentic dialogue. Otherwise, we fail to understand the thinking of others, or to realize deep down that the brother or sister we wish to reach and redeem, with the power and the closeness of love, counts more than their positions, distant as they may be from what we hold as true and certain. Harsh and divisive language does not befit the tongue of a pastor, it has no place in his heart; although it may momentarily seem to win the day, only the enduring allure of goodness and love remains truly convincing.

We need to let the Lord's words echo constantly in our hearts: "*Take my yoke upon you, and learn from me, who am meek and humble of heart, and you will find refreshment for your souls*" (Mt 11:28-30). Jesus' yoke is a yoke of love and thus a pledge of refreshment. At times in our work we can be burdened by a sense of loneliness, and so feel the heaviness of the yoke that we forget that we have received it from the Lord. It seems to be ours alone, and so we drag it like weary oxen working a dry field, troubled by the thought that we are laboring in vain. We can forget the profound refreshment which is indissolubly linked to the One who has made us the promise.

We need to learn from Jesus, or better to learn Jesus, meek and humble; to enter into his meekness and his humility by contemplating his way of acting; to lead our Churches and our people—not infrequently burdened by the stress of everyday life—to the ease of the Lord's yoke. And to remember that Jesus' Church is kept whole not by "*consuming fire from heaven*" (Lk 9.54), but by the secret warmth of the Spirit, who "*heals what is wounded, bends what is rigid, straightens what is crooked.*"

The great mission which the Lord gives us is one which we carry out in communion, collegially. The world is already so torn and divided, brokenness is now everywhere. Consequently, the Church, "*the seamless garment of the Lord*" cannot allow herself to be rent, broken or fought over.

Our mission as bishops is first and foremost to solidify unity, a unity whose content is defined by the Word of God and the one Bread of Heaven. With these two realities each of the Churches entrusted to us remains Catholic, because open to, and in communion with, all the particular Churches and with the Church of Rome which "*presides in charity.*" It is imperative, therefore, to watch over that unity, to safeguard it, to promote it and to bear witness to it as a sign and instrument which, beyond every barrier, unites nations, races, classes and generations. . . .

Be pastors close to people, pastors who are neighbors and servants. Let this closeness be expressed in a special way toward your priests. Support them, so that they can continue to serve Christ with an undivided heart, for this alone can bring fulfillment to ministers of Christ. I urge you, then, not to let them be content with half-measures. Find ways to encourage their spiritual growth, lest they yield to the temptation to become notaries and bureaucrats, but instead reflect the motherhood of the Church, which gives birth to and raises her sons and daughters. Be vigilant lest they tire of getting up to answer those who knock on their door by night, just when they feel entitled to rest (Lk 11:5-8). Train them to be ready to stop, care for, soothe, lift up and assist those who, "*by chance*" find themselves stripped of all they thought they had (Lk 10:29-37).

Do Not Fear Transparency

Meeting with the Bishops of Mexico

Mexico City, February 13, 2016

Dear Brothers,

I am pleased to have this opportunity of meeting you the day after my arrival here in this country, which, following in the footsteps of my predecessors, I also have come to visit.

How could I not come! Could the Successor of Peter, called from the far south of Latin America, deprive himself of seeing *la Virgen Morenita*?

I thank you for receiving me in this Cathedral, a larger *casita* ("little home") and yet always *sagrada* ("sacred"), as the Blessed Virgin of Guadalupe had requested. I also thank you for your kind words of welcome.

I know that here is found the secret heart of each Mexican, and I enter with soft footsteps as is fitting for one who enters the home and soul of this people; and I am deeply grateful to you for having opened your doors to me. I know that by looking into the eyes of the Blessed Virgin I am able to follow the gaze of your sons and daughters who, in her, have learned to express themselves. I know that no other voice can speak so powerfully to me of the Mexican heart as the Blessed Mother can; she guards its highest aspirations and most hidden hopes; she gathers its joys and its tears. She understands its various languages and she responds with a Mother's tenderness because these men and women are her own children.

I am happy to be with you here, near *Cerro del Tepeyac*, in a way close to the dawn of evangelization in this continent. Please allow *la Guadalupana* to be the starting point of everything I will say to you. How I wish She herself would convey to you all that is dear to the Pope's heart, reaching the depths of your own pastoral hearts, and through you, to each of the particular Churches present in this vast country of Mexico.

The Pope for some time has nourished a desire to see *la Guadalupana* just as St. Juan Diego did, and successive generations of children after him. And I have desired, even more, to be captured by her maternal gaze. I have reflected greatly on the mystery of this gaze and I ask you to receive in these moments what pours forth from my heart, the heart of a Pastor.

A GAZE OF TENDERNESS

Above all, *la Virgen Morenita* teaches us that the only power capable of conquering the hearts of men and women is the tenderness of God. That which delights and attracts, that which humbles and overcomes, that which opens and unleashes, is not the power of instruments or the force of law, but rather the omnipotent weakness of divine love, which is the irresistible force of its gentleness and the irrevocable pledge of its mercy.

A rather inquisitive and famous literary figure of yours, Octavio Paz, said that in Guadalupe great harvests and fertile lands are no longer prayed for, but instead a place of rest where people, still orphaned and disinherited, may seek a place of refuge, a home.

With centuries having gone by since the founding event of this country and the evangelization of the continent, it may be asked: Has the need been diluted or even forgotten for that place of rest so ardently desired by the hearts of Mexicans entrusted to your care?

I know the long and painful history which you have gone through has not been without much bloodshed, impetuous and heartbreaking upheavals, violence and incomprehension. With good reason my venerable and saintly predecessor, who felt at home here in Mexico, wished to remind us: "Like rivers that are sometimes hidden and plentiful, converge at times and at others reveal their complementary differences, without ever merging completely: the ancient and rich sensitivity of the indigenous peoples loved by Juan de Zumárraga and Vasco de Quiroga, whom many of these peoples continue to call fathers; Christianity, rooted in the Mexican soul; and modern rationality of the European kind, which wanted so much to exalt independence and freedom" (John Paul II, Address, Welcoming Ceremony, January 22, 1999).

And in this history, the maternal place of rest which continually brought life to Mexico, although sometimes seeming like "a net of a hundred and fifty-three fish" (cf. Jn 21:11), was never without fruit, was always able to heal the divisions which threatened.

161

For this reason I invite you to begin anew from that need for a place of rest which wells up from the spirit of your people. The restful place of the Christian faith is capable of reconciling a past, often marked by loneliness, isolation and rejection, with a future, continually relegated to a tomorrow which just slips away. Only in that place of faith can we, without renouncing our own identity, discover "the profound truth of the new humanity, in which all are called to be children of God" (John Paul II, Homily, Canonization of Juan Diego, July 31, 2002).

Bow down then brothers, quietly and respectfully, toward the profound spirit of your people, bow down with care and decipher its mysterious face. The present, so often mixed with dispersion and festivity, is it perhaps not for God a preparatory stage, for him who alone is fully present? Familiarity with pain and death, is it not a form of courage and pathway to hope? And the view that the world is always and uniquely in need of redemption, is this not an antidote to the proud self-sufficiency of those who think they can do without God?

Naturally, for this reason it is necessary to have an outlook capable of reflecting the tenderness of God. I ask you, therefore, to be bishops who have a pure vision, a transparent soul, and a joyful face. Do not fear transparency. The Church does not need darkness to carry out her work. Be vigilant so that your vision will not be darkened by the gloomy mist of worldliness; do not allow yourselves to be corrupted by trivial materialism or by the seductive illusion of underhanded agreements; do not place your faith in the "chariots and horses" of today's pharaohs, for our strength is in "the pillar of fire" which divides the sea in two, without much fanfare (cf. Ex 14:24-25).

The world in which the Lord calls us to carry out our mission has become extremely complicated. And even the proud notion of *cogito*, which at least did not deny that there was a rock on the sand of being, is today dominated by a view of life which, now more than ever, many consider to be hesitant, itinerant and lawless because it lacks a firm foundation. Frontiers so passionately invoked and upheld are now open to the irony of a world in which the power of some can no longer survive without the vulnerability of others. The irreversible hybridization of technology brings closer what is distant; sadly, however, it also distances what should be close.

And it is in this very world, as it is, that God asks you to have a view capable of grasping that plea which cries out from the heart of your people, a plea which has its own calendar day, the *Feast of Crying Out*. This cry needs a response: God exists and is close in Jesus Christ. God is the only reality upon which we can build, because, "God is the foundational reality, not a God who is merely imagined or hypothetical, but God with a human face" (Benedict XVI, Address to CELAM, May 13, 2007).

Observing your faces, the Mexican people have the right to witness the signs of those "who have seen the Lord" (cf. Jn 20:25), of those who have been with God. This is essential. Therefore, do not lose time or energy in secondary things, in gossip or intrigue, in conceited schemes of careerism, in empty plans for superiority, in unproductive groups that seek benefits or common interests. Do not allow yourselves to be dragged into gossip and slander. Introduce your priests into a correct understanding of sacred ministry. For us ministers of God it is enough to have the grace to "drink the cup of the Lord," the gift of protecting that portion of the heritage which has been entrusted to us, though we may be unskilled administrators. Let us allow the Father to assign the place he has prepared for us (Mt 20:20-28). Can we really be concerned with affairs that are not the Father's? Away from the "Father's affairs" (Lk 2:48-49) we lose our identity and, through our own fault, empty his grace of meaning.

If our vision does not witness to having seen Jesus, then the words with which we recall him will be rhetorical and empty figures of speech. They may perhaps express the nostalgia of those who cannot forget the Lord, but who have become, at any rate, mere babbling orphans beside a tomb. Finally, they may be words that are incapable of preventing this world of ours from being abandoned and reduced to its own desperate power.

I think of the need to offer a maternal place of rest to young people. May your vision be capable of meeting theirs, loving them and understanding what they search for with that energy that inspired many like them to leave behind their boats and nets on the other side of the sea (Mk 1:17-18), to leave the abuses of the banking sector so as to follow the Lord on the path of true wealth (cf. Mt 9:9).

I am concerned about those many persons who, seduced by the empty power of the world, praise illusions and embrace their macabre symbols to commercialize death in exchange for money which, in the end, "moth and rust consume" and "thieves break in and steal" (Mt 6:19). I urge you not to underestimate the moral and antisocial challenge which the drug trade represents for the youth and for Mexican society as a whole, as well as for the Church.

The magnitude of this phenomenon, the complexity of its causes, its immensity and its scope which devours like a metastasis, and the gravity of the violence which divides with its distorted expressions, do not allow us as Pastors of the Church to hide behind anodyne denunciations—forms of abstract thinking. Rather they demand of us a prophetic courage as well as a reliable and qualified pastoral plan, so that we can gradually help build that fragile network of human relationships without which all of us would be defeated from the outset in the face of such an insidious threat. Only by starting with families, by drawing close and embracing the fringes of human existence in the ravaged areas of our cities and by seeking the involvement of parish communities, schools, community institutions, political communities and institutions responsible for security, will people finally escape the raging waters that drown so many, either victims of the drug trade or those who stand before God with their hands drenched in blood, though with pockets filled with sordid money and their consciences deadened. Returning to the gaze of Mary of Guadalupe, I want to add a second consideration:

A CONSTRUCTIVE VISION

In the mantle of the Mexican spirit, with the thread of *mestizo* characteristics, God has woven and revealed in *la Morenita* the face of the Mexican people. God does not need subdued colors to design this face, for his designs are not conditioned by colors or threads but rather by the permanence of his love which constantly desires to imprint itself upon us.

Therefore, be bishops who are capable of imitating this freedom of God who chooses the humble in order to reveal the majesty of his countenance; capable of reproducing this divine patience by weaving the new man which your country awaits with the fine thread made of the men and women you encounter. Do not be led by empty efforts to change people as if the love of God is not powerful enough to bring about change.

Rediscover the wise and humble constancy that the Fathers of faith of this country passed on to successive generations with the language of divine mystery. They did this by first learning and then teaching the grammar needed to dialogue with God; a God concealed within centuries of searching and then brought close in the person of his Son Jesus Christ, who is our future and who is recognized as such by so many men and women when they behold his bloody and humiliated face. Imitate his gracious humility and his bowing down to help us. We will never comprehend sufficiently how, with the *mestizo* threads of our people, God has woven the face by which he is to be known. We can never be thankful enough for this bowing down, for this "*sincatábasis*."

I ask you to show singular tenderness in the way you regard indigenous peoples, them and their fascinating but not infrequently decimated cultures. Mexico needs its American-Indian roots so as not to remain an unresolved enigma. The indigenous people of Mexico still await true recognition of the richness of their contribution and the fruitfulness of their presence. In this way they can inherit that identity which transforms them into a single nation and not only an identity among other identities.

On many occasions, much has been said about a supposedly failed future of this nation, about a *labyrinth of loneliness* in which it is imprisoned by its geography as well as by a fate which has ensnared it. For some, all of this is an obstacle to the plan for a unified face, an adult identity, a unique position among the concert of nations and a shared mission.

For others, the Church in Mexico is also regarded as being either condemned to suffer the inferior position to which it was relegated in some periods of its past, as for example when its voice was silenced and efforts were made to eradicate it; or condemned to venture into expressions of fundamentalism thus holding onto provisional certainties—as that famous *cogito*—while forgetting to have in its heart the thirst for the Absolute and be called in Christ to unite everyone and not just a portion (cf. *Lumen Gentium*, no. 1).

On the other hand, never cease to remind your people of how powerful their ancient roots are, roots which have allowed a vibrant Christian synthesis of human, cultural and spiritual unity which was forged here. Remember that the wings of your people have spread on various occasions to rise above changing situations. Protect the memory of the long journey undertaken so far—be *deuteronomical*—and know how to inspire the hope of attaining new heights because the future will bear a land "rich in fruit" even if it involves considerable challenges (Nm 13:27-28).

May your vision, always and solely resting upon Christ, be capable of contributing to the unity of the people in your care; of favoring the reconciliation of its differences and the integration of its diversities; of promoting a solution to its endogenous problems; of remembering the high standards which Mexico can attain when it learns to belong to itself rather than to others; of helping to find shared and sustainable solutions to its misfortunes; of motivating the entire nation to not be content with less than what is expected of a Mexican way of living in the world. A third thought:

A VISION THAT IS CLOSE AND ATTENTIVE, NOT DORMANT

I urge you to not fall into that paralyzation of standard responses to new questions. Your past is a source of riches to be mined and which can inspire the present and illumine the future. How unfortunate you are if you rest on your laurels! It is important not to squander the inheritance you have received by protecting it through constant work. You stand on the shoulders of giants: bishops, priests, religious and lay faithful "unto the end," who have offered their lives so that the Church can fulfill her own mission. From those heights you are called to turn your gaze to the Lord's vineyard to plan the sowing and wait for the harvest.

I invite you to give yourselves tirelessly, tirelessly and fearlessly to the task of evangelizing and deepening the faith by means of a myst-agogical catechesis that treasures the popular religiosity of the people. Our times require pastoral attention to persons and groups who hope to encounter the living Jesus. Only the courageous pastoral conversion—and I underline pastoral conversion—of our communities can seek, generate and nourish today's disciples of the Lord (cf. *Aparecida*, 226, 368, 370).

Hence it is necessary for us Pastors to overcome the temptation of aloofness—and I leave it up to each of you to list the kinds of aloofness that can exist in this Episcopal Conference; I do not know them, but it is important to overcome this temptation—and clericalism, of coldness and indifference, of triumphalism and self-centeredness. Guadalupe teaches us that God is known, and is closer to us, by his countenance and that closeness and humility, that bowing down and drawing close, are more powerful than force.

As the wonderful *Guadalupana* tradition teaches us, *la Morenita* gathers together those who contemplate her, and reflects the faces of those who find her. It is essential to learn that there is something unique in every person who looks to us in their search for God. We must guard against becoming impervious to such gazes but rather gather them to our hearts and guard them.

Only a Church able to shelter the faces of men and women who knock on her doors will be able to speak to them of God. If we do not know how to decipher their sufferings, if we do not come to understand their needs, then we can offer them nothing. The richness we have flows only when we encounter the smallness of those who beg and this encounter occurs precisely in our hearts, the hearts of Pastors.

And the first face I ask you to guard in your hearts is that of your priests. Do not leave them exposed to loneliness and abandonment, easy prey to a worldliness that devours the heart. Be attentive and learn how to read their expressions so as to rejoice with them when they feel the joy of recounting all that they have "done and taught" (Mk 6:30). Also, do not step back when they feel humiliated and can only cry because they "have denied the Lord" (cf. Lk 22:61-62), and, why not also offer your support, in communion with Christ, when one of them, already disheartened, goes out with Judas into "the night" (cf. Jn 13:30). As bishops in these situations, your paternal care for your priests must never be found wanting. Encourage communion among them; seek the perfection of their gifts; involve them in great ventures, for the heart of an apostle was not made for small things.

The need for familiarity abides in the heart of God. Our Lady of Guadalupe therefore asks for a *casita sagrada*, a "small holy home." Our Latin American populations know well the diminutive forms of expression—a *casita sagrada*—and use them willingly. Perhaps they need to use the diminutive forms because they would feel lost otherwise. They have adapted themselves to feeling small and have grown accustomed to living modestly.

When the Church congregates in a majestic Cathedral, she should not fail to see herself as a "small home" in which her children can feel comfortable. We remain in God's presence only when we are little ones, orphans and beggars. The actors in the history of salvation are beggars.

A "small home," *casita*, is familiar and at the same time "holy," *sagrada*, for it is filled by God's omnipotent greatness. We are guardians of this mystery. Perhaps we have lost the sense of the humble ways of the divine and are tired of offering our own men and women the *casita* in which they feel close to God. On occasion, a disregard for the sense of omnipotent greatness has led to a partial loss of reverential fear toward such great love. Where God lives, man cannot enter without being invited in and he can only enter "taking off his shoes" (cf. Ex 3:5), so as to confess his unworthiness.

Our having forgotten this "taking off our shoes" in order to enter: is this perhaps not the root cause of that lost sense of the sacredness of human life, of the person, of fundamental values, of the wisdom accumulated along the centuries, and of respect for the environment? Without rescuing within the consciences of men and women and of society these profound roots and the generous efforts to promote legitimate human rights, the vital sap will be lacking; and it is a sap that comes only from a source which humanity itself cannot procure. And, always with eyes on Mary, I conclude with a final thought:

A HOLISTIC AND UNIFIED VISION

Only by looking at la *Morenita* can Mexico be understood in its entirety. And so I invite you to appreciate that the mission, which the Church today entrusts to you, demands, and has always done so, a vision embracing the whole. This cannot be realized in an isolated manner, but only in communion.

La Guadalupana has a ribbon around her waist which proclaims her fecundity. She is the Blessed Virgin who already has in her womb the Son awaited by men and women. She is the Mother who already carries the humanity of a newborn world. She is the Bride who prefigures the maternal fruitfulness of Christ's Church. You have been entrusted with the mission of enrobing the Mexican nation with God's fruitfulness. No part of this ribbon can be despised.

The Mexican episcopate has made significant strides in these years since the Council; it has increased its members; it has promoted permanent formation which is consistent and professional; there has been a fraternal atmosphere; the spirit of collegiality has matured; the pastoral efforts have had an influence on your local Churches and on the conscience of the nation, the shared pastoral initiatives have been fruitful in vital areas of the Church's mission, such as the family, vocations, and the Church's presence in society.

While we are encouraged by the path taken during these years, I would ask you not to lose heart in the face of difficulties and not to spare any effort in promoting, among yourselves and in your dioceses, a missionary zeal, especially toward the most needy areas of the one body of the Mexican Church. To rediscover that the Church *is mission* is fundamental for her future, because only the "enthusiasm and confident admiration" of evangelizers has the power to attract. I ask you, therefore, to take great care in forming and preparing the lay-faithful, overcoming all forms of clericalism and involving them actively in the mission of the Church, above all making the Gospel of Christ present in the world by personal witness.

Of great benefit to the Mexican people will be the unifying witness of the Christian synthesis and the shared vision of the identity and future of its people. In this sense, it is important for the Pontifical University of Mexico to be increasingly involved in the efforts of the Church to ensure a universal perspective; for without this, reason, which tends to compartmentalize, will renounce its highest ideal of seeking the truth.

The mission is vast, and to carry it forward requires multiple paths. I strongly reiterate my appeal to you to preserve the communion and unity that exist among you. This is essential, brothers. These words are not in my text but come spontaneously: If you must argue, argue; if you have to say things, say them; but say them as men, face to face, and as men of God who then go to pray together and discern together. And if you have gone too far, then ask for forgiveness, but always maintain the unity of the episcopal body: communion and unity among yourselves. Communion is the essential form of the Church, and the unity of her Pastors offers proof of its truth. Mexico and its vast, multifaceted Church, stand in need of bishops who are servants and custodians of that unity built on the Word of God, nourished by his Body and guided by his Spirit who is the life-giving breath of the Church.

We do not need "princes," but rather a community of the Lord's witnesses. Christ is the only light; he is the wellspring of living water; from his breath comes forth the Spirit, who fills the sails of the ecclesial bark. In the glorified Christ, whom the people of this country love to honor as King, may you together kindle and be filled by the light of his presence which is never extinguished; breathe deeply the wholesome air of his Spirit. It falls to you to sow Christ in this land, to keep alive his humble light which enlightens without causing confusion, to ensure that in his living waters the thirst of your people is quenched; to set the sails so that the Spirit's breeze may fill them, never allowing the bark of the Church in Mexico to run aground.

Remember: the Bride, the Bride of each of you, the Mother Church, knows that the beloved Pastor (cf. Song 1:7) will be found only where there are verdant pastures and crystal clear streams. She does not trust those companions of the Bridegroom who, sometimes out of laziness or inability, lead the sheep through arid lands and areas strewn with rocks. Woe to us pastors, companions of the Supreme Pastor, if we allow his Bride to wander because we have set up tents where the Bridegroom cannot be found!

Allow me a final word to convey the appreciation of the Pope for everything you are doing to confront the challenge of our age: migration. There are millions of sons and daughters of the Church who today live in the diaspora or who are in transit, journeying to the north in search of new opportunities. Many of them have left behind their roots in order to brave the future, even in clandestine conditions which involve so many risks; they do this to seek the "green light" which they regard as hope. So many families are separated; and integration into a supposed "promised land" is not always as easy as some believe.

Brothers, may your hearts be capable of following these men and women and reaching them beyond the borders. Strengthen the communion with your brothers of the North American episcopate, so that the maternal presence of the Church can keep alive the roots of the faith, the faith of that people, and the motivation for their hope and the power of their charity. May it never happen to them, that, hanging up their lyres, their joys become dampened, they forget Jerusalem and are exiled from themselves (cf. Ps 136). I ask you to witness together that the Church is the custodian of a unifying vision of humanity and that she cannot consent to being reduced to a mere human "resource."

Your efforts will not be in vain when your dioceses show care by pouring balm on the injured feet of those who walk through your territories, sharing with them the resources collected through the sacrifices of many; the divine Samaritan in the end will enrich the person who is not indifferent to him as he lies on the side of the road (cf. Lk 10:25-37).

Dear brothers, the Pope is sure that Mexico and its Church will make it in time to that rendezvous with themselves, with history and with God. Perhaps some stone on the way may slow their pace and the struggle of the journey may call for rest, but nothing will make them lose sight of the destination. For how can someone arrive late when it is their mother who is waiting? Who is unable to hear within themselves that voice, "Am I not here, I who am your Mother?" Thank you.

Christmas Greetings from
the Roman Curia

Professionalism, Service, and Holiness

Clementine Hall, December 21, 2013

The Lord has enabled us to journey through Advent, and all too quickly we have come to these final days before Christmas. They are days marked by a unique spiritual climate made up of emotions, memories and signs, both liturgical and otherwise, such as the crèche. . . . It is in this climate that this traditional meeting takes place with you, the Superiors and Officials of the Roman Curia, who cooperate daily in the service of the Church. I greet all of you with affection. Allow me to extend a special greeting to Archbishop Pietro Parolin, who recently began his service as Secretary of State, and who needs our prayers!

While our hearts are full of gratitude to God, who so loved us that he gave us his only-begotten Son, it is also good to make room for gratitude to one another. In this, my first Christmas as the Bishop of Rome, I also feel the need to offer sincere thanks to all of you as a community of service, and to each of you individually. I thank you for the work which you do each day: for the care, diligence and creativity which you display; and for your effort—I know it is not always easy—to work together in the office, both to listen to and challenge one another, and to bring out the best in all your different personalities and gifts, in a spirit of mutual respect.

In a particular way, I want to express my gratitude to those now concluding their service and approaching retirement. As priests and bishops, we know full well that we never really retire, but we do leave the office, and rightly so, not least to devote ourselves a little more fully to prayer and the care of souls, starting with our own! So a very special and heartfelt "thank you" goes to those of you who have worked here for so many years with immense dedication, hidden from the eyes of the world. This is something truly admirable. I have such high regard for these "Monsignori" who are cut from the same mold as the *curiales* of olden times, exemplary persons. . . . We need them today, too! People who work with competence, precision and self-sacrifice in the fulfillment of their daily duties. Here I would like to mention some of them by name, as a way of expressing my esteem and my gratitude, but we know that, in any list, the first names people notice are the ones that are missing! Besides, I would also risk overlooking someone and thus committing an injustice and a lack of charity. But I want to say to these brothers of ours that they offer a very important witness in the Church's journey through history.

They are also an example, and their example and their witness make me think of two hallmarks of the curial official, and even more of curial superiors, which I would like to emphasize: professionalism and service.

Professionalism, by which I mean competence, study, keeping abreast of things. . . . This is a basic requisite for working in the Curia. Naturally, professionalism is something which develops, and is in part acquired; but I think that, precisely for it to develop and to be acquired, there has to be a good foundation from the outset.

The second hallmark is service: service to the Pope and to the bishops, to the universal Church and to the particular Churches. In the Roman Curia, one learns—in a special way, "one breathes in"—this twofold aspect of the Church, this interplay of the universal and the particular. I think that this is one of the finest experiences of those who live and work in Rome: "to sense" the Church in this way. When professionalism is lacking, there is a slow drift downward toward mediocrity. Dossiers become full of trite and lifeless information, and incapable of opening up lofty perspectives. Then too, when the attitude is no longer one of service to the particular Churches and their bishops, the structure of the Curia turns into a ponderous, bureaucratic customhouse, constantly inspecting and questioning, hindering the working of the Holy Spirit and the growth of God's people.

To these two qualities of professionalism and service, I would also like to add a third, which is holiness of life. We know very well that, in the hierarchy of values, this is the most important. Indeed, it is basic for the quality of our work, our service. Here I would like to say that in the Roman Curia there have been, and still are, saints. I have said this publicly on more than one occasion, as a way of thanking the Lord. Holiness means a life immersed in the Spirit, a heart open to God, constant prayer, deep humility and fraternal charity in our relationships with our fellow workers. It also means apostleship, discreet and faithful pastoral service, zealously carried out in direct contact with God's people. For priests, this is indispensable.

Holiness, in the Curia, also means conscientious objection. Yes, conscientious objection to gossip! We rightfully insist on the importance of conscientious objection, but perhaps we too need to exercise it as a means of defending ourselves from an unwritten law of our surroundings, which unfortunately is that of gossip. So let us all be conscientious objectors; and mind you, I am not simply preaching! For gossip is harmful to people, harmful to our work and our surroundings.

Dear brothers and sisters, let us feel close to one another on this final stretch of the road to Bethlehem. We would do well to meditate on St. Joseph, who was so silent yet so necessary at the side of Our Lady. Let us think about him and his loving concern for his Spouse and for the Baby Jesus. This can tell us a lot about our own service to the Church! So let us experience this Christmas in spiritual closeness to St. Joseph. This will benefit all of us!

I thank you most heartily for your work and especially for your prayers. Truly I feel "borne aloft" by your prayers and I ask you to continue to support me in this way. I too remember you before the Lord, and I impart my blessing as I offer my best wishes for a Christmas filled with light and peace for each of you and for all your dear ones. Happy Christmas!

The Roman Curia and the Body of Christ

Clementine Hall, December 22, 2014

"You are higher than the cherubim, you who changed the pitiful plight of the world when you became like one of us." (St. Athanasius)

Dear Brothers and Sisters,

At the end of Advent, we meet for our traditional greetings. In a few days we will have the joy of celebrating the birth of the Lord: the event of God who became man in order to save us; the manifestation of the love of God who does not just give us something, or send us a message or a few messengers, but gives us himself; the mystery of God who took upon himself our humanity and our sins in order to reveal his divine life, his immense grace and his freely-given forgiveness. It is our encounter with God who is born in the poverty of the stable of Bethlehem in order to teach us the power of humility. For Christmas is also the feast of the light which is not received by the "chosen," but by the poor and simple who awaited the salvation of the Lord.

Before all else, I would like to offer all of you—coworkers, brothers and sisters, papal representatives throughout the world, and all your dear ones—my prayerful good wishes for a holy Christmas and a happy New Year. I want to thank you most heartily for your daily commitment in the service of the Holy See, the Catholic Church, the particular Churches and the Successor of Peter.

Since we are persons and not numbers or mere titles, I would mention in a particular way those who in the course of this year concluded their service for reasons of age, or the assumption of new duties, or because they were called to the house of the Father. My thoughts and my gratitude go to them and to their families.

Together with you, I want to lift up to the Lord a lively and heartfelt thanksgiving for the year now ending, for all we have experienced, and for all the good which he has graciously willed to accomplish through our service of the Holy See, while at the same time humbly begging his forgiveness for our failings committed *"in our thoughts and words, in what we have done and what we have failed to do."*

Taking this request for forgiveness as my starting point, I would like this meeting and the reflections which I will now share with you to be for all of us a help and a stimulus to a true examination of conscience, in order to prepare our hearts for the holy feast of Christmas.

As I thought about this meeting, there came to mind the image of the Church as the Mystical Body of Jesus Christ. This is an expression which, as Pope Pius XII explained, "springs up and in some way blossoms from the frequent teaching of sacred Scripture and the Fathers of the Church."[1] As St. Paul wrote: "For just as the body is one and has many members, and all the members of the body, though many, are one body, so it is with Christ" (1 Cor 12:12).[2]

The Second Vatican Council thus recalls that "a diversity of members and functions is engaged in the building up of Christ's body too, There is only one Spirit who, out of his own richness and the needs of the ministries, gives his various gifts for the welfare of the Church (cf. 1 Cor 12:1-11).[3] As a result, "Christ and the Church together make up the 'whole Christ' (*Christus totus*). The Church is one with Christ."[4]

It is attractive to think of the Roman Curia as a small-scale model of the Church, in other words, as a "body" which strives seriously every day

---

1   He states that the Church, being *mysticum Corpus Christi*, "calls also for a multiplicity of members, which are linked together in such a way as to help one another. As in the body, when one member suffers, all the other members share its pain, and the healthy members come to the aid of the ailing, so in the Church the individual members do not live for themselves alone, but also help their fellows, and all work in mutual collaboration for the common comfort and for the more perfect building up of the whole Body . . . a Body not formed by a haphazard grouping of members, but . . . constituted of organs, that is of members, that have not the same function and are arranged in due order; so for this reason above all the Church is called a body, that it is constituted by the coalescence of structurally united parts" (Encyclical *Mystici Corporis*, Part One: AAS 35 [1943], 200; ed. Carlen, nos. 15-16).

2   Cf. Rom 12:5: "So we, though many, are one body in Christ, and individually members of one another."

3   Dogmatic Constitution *Lumen Gentium*, no. 7.

4   It should be remembered that "the comparison of the Church with the body casts light on the intimae bond between Christ and his Church. Not only is she gathered *around him*; she is united *in him*, in his body. Three aspects of the Church as the body of Christ are to be more specifically noted: *the unity of all her members with each other as a result of their union with Christ; Christ as the head of the body; and the Church as bride of Christ*. Cf. *Catechism of the Catholic Church*, nos. 789 and 795.

to be more alive, more healthy, more harmonious and more united in itself and with Christ.

In fact, though, the Roman Curia is a complex body, made up of a number of Congregations, Councils, Offices, Tribunals, Commissions, as of numerous elements which do not all have the same task but are coordinated in view of an effective, edifying, disciplined and exemplary functioning, notwithstanding the cultural, linguistic and national differences of its members.[5]

However, since the Curia is a dynamic body, it cannot live without nourishment and care. In fact, the Curia—like the Church—cannot live without a vital, personal, authentic and solid relationship with Christ.[6] A member of the Curia who is not daily nourished by that Food will become a bureaucrat (a formalist, a functionalist, a mere employee): a branch which withers, slowly dies and is then cast off. Daily prayer, assiduous reception of the sacraments, particularly the Eucharist and Reconciliation, daily contact with the word of God and a spirituality which translates into lived charity—these are vital nourishment for each of us. Let it be clear to all of us that apart from him we can do nothing (cf. Jn 15:8).

As a result, a living relationship with God also nourishes and strengthens our communion with others. In other words, the more closely we are joined to God, the more we are united among ourselves, since *the Spirit of God unites and the spirit of evil divides.*

The Curia is called constantly to improve and to grow in *communion, holiness and wisdom*, in order to carry out fully its mission.[7] And yet, like any body, like any human body, it is also exposed to diseases, malfunctioning, infirmity. Here I would like to mention some of these probable diseases, "curial diseases." They are the more common diseases in our life in the Curia. They are diseases and temptations which weaken our service to the Lord. I think a "listing" of these diseases—along the lines of the Desert Fathers who used to draw up such lists—will help us

---

5   Cf. *Evangelii Gaudium*, nos. 130-131.

6   Jesus often spoke of the union which the faithful should have with him: "As the branch cannot bear fruit by itself, unless it abides in the vine, neither can you, unless you abide in me" (Jn 15:4-5).

7   Cf. *Pastor Bonus*, Art. 1, and CIC, c. 360.

to prepare for the sacrament of Reconciliation, which will be a good step for all of us to take in preparing for Christmas.

1. The disease of thinking we are "immortal," "immune" or downright "indispensable," neglecting the need for regular check-ups. A Curia which is not *self-critical*, which does not keep up with things, which does not seek to be more fit, is a sick body. A simple visit to the cemetery might help us see the names of many people who thought they were immortal, immune and indispensable! It is the disease of the rich fool in the Gospel, who thought he would live forever (cf. Lk 12:13-21), but also of those who turn into lords and masters, and think of themselves as above others and not at their service. It is often an effect of the pathology of power, from a superiority complex, from a narcissism which passionately gazes at its own image and does not see the image of God on the face of others, especially the weakest and those most in need.[8] The antidote to this plague is the grace of realizing that we are sinners and able to say heartily: "We are unworthy servants. We have only done what was our duty" (Lk 17:10).

2. Another disease is the "Martha complex," excessive busyness. It is found in those who immerse themselves in work and inevitably neglect *"the better part"*: sitting at the feet of Jesus (cf. Lk 10:38-42). Jesus called his disciples to *"rest a while"* (cf. Mk 6:31) for a reason, because neglecting needed rest leads to stress and agitation. A time of rest, for those who have completed their work, is necessary, obligatory and should be taken seriously: by spending time with one's family and respecting holidays as moments of spiritual and physical recharging. We need to learn from Qohelet that "for everything there is a season" (3:1-15).

3. Then too there is the disease of mental and spiritual "petrification." It is found in those who have a heart of stone, the "stiff-necked" (Acts 7:51-60), in those who in the course of time lose their interior serenity, alertness and daring, and hide under a pile of papers, turning into *paper pushers* and not *men of God* (cf. Heb 3:12). It is dangerous to lose the human sensitivity that enables us to weep with those who weep and to rejoice with those who rejoice! This is the disease of those who lose *"the sentiments of Jesus"* (cf. Phil 2:5-11), because as time goes on their hearts grow hard and become incapable of loving unconditionally the Father and our neighbor (cf. Mt 22:34-35). Being a Christian means

---

8   Cf. *Evangelii Gaudium*, nos. 197-201.

"having the same sentiments that were in Christ Jesus" (Phil 2:5), sentiments of humility and unselfishness, of detachment and generosity.[9]

4. The disease of excessive planning and of functionalism. When the apostle plans everything down to the last detail and believes that with perfect planning things will fall into place, he becomes an accountant or an office manager. Things need to be prepared well, but without ever falling into the temptation of trying to contain and direct the freedom of the Holy Spirit, which is always greater and more flexible than any human planning (cf. Jn 3:8). We contract this disease because "it is always more easy and comfortable to settle in our own sedentary and unchanging ways. In truth, the Church shows her fidelity to the Holy Spirit to the extent that she does not try to control or tame him . . . to tame the Holy Spirit! . . . He is freshness, imagination, and newness."[10]

5. The disease of poor coordination. Once its members lose communion among themselves, the body loses its harmonious functioning and its equilibrium; it then becomes an orchestra which produces noise: its members do not work together and lose the spirit of fellowship and teamwork. When the foot says to the arm: "I don't need you," or the hand says to the head, "I'm in charge," they create discomfort and scandal.

6. There is also a "spiritual Alzheimer's disease." It consists in losing the memory of our personal "salvation history," our past history with the Lord and our "first love" (Rev 2:4). It involves a progressive decline in the spiritual faculties which in the long or short run greatly handicaps a person by making him incapable of doing anything on his own, living in a state of absolute dependence on his often imaginary perceptions. We see it in those who have lost the memory of their encounter with the Lord; in those who no longer see life's meaning in "deuteronomic" terms; in those who are completely caught up in the present moment, in their passions, whims and obsessions; in those who build walls and routines around themselves, and thus become more and more the slaves of idols carved by their own hands.

7. The disease of rivalry and vainglory.[11] When appearances, the color of our clothes and our titles of honor become the primary object in

---

9   Pope Benedict XVI, General Audience, June 1, 2005.

10   Pope Francis, Homily at Mass in Turkey, November 29, 2014.

11   Cf. *Evangelii Gaudium*, nos. 95-96.

life, we forget the words of St. Paul: "*Do nothing from selfishness or conceit but in humility count others better than yourselves. Let each of you look not only to his own interests, but also to the interests of others*" (Phil 2:3-4). This is a disease which leads us to be men and woman of deceit, and to live a false "mysticism" and a false "quietism." St. Paul himself defines such persons as "*enemies of the cross of Christ*" because "they glory in their shame, with minds set on earthly things" (Phil 3:19).

8. The disease of existential schizophrenia. This is the disease of those who live a double life, the fruit of that hypocrisy typical of the mediocre and of a progressive spiritual emptiness which no doctorates or academic titles can fill. It is a disease which often strikes those who abandon pastoral service and restrict themselves to bureaucratic matters, thus losing contact with reality, with concrete people. In this way they create their own parallel world, where they set aside all that they teach with severity to others and begin to live a hidden and often dissolute life. For this most serious disease conversion is most urgent and indeed indispensable (cf. Lk 15:11-32).

9. The disease of gossiping, grumbling and back-biting. I have already spoken many times about this disease, but never enough. It is a grave illness which begins simply, perhaps even in small talk, and takes over a person, making him become a "*sower of weeds*" (like Satan) and in many cases, a cold-blooded killer of the good name of our colleagues and confrères. It is the disease of cowardly persons who lack the courage to speak out directly, but instead speak behind other people's backs. St. Paul admonishes us to "*do all things without grumbling or questioning, that you may be blameless and innocent*" (Phil 2:14-15). Brothers, let us be on our guard against the terrorism of gossip!

10. The disease of idolizing superiors. This is the disease of those who court their superiors in the hope of gaining their favor. They are victims of careerism and opportunism; they honor persons and not God (cf. Mt 23:8-12). They serve thinking only of what they can get and not of what they should give. Small-minded persons, unhappy and inspired only by their own lethal selfishness (cf. Gal 5:16-25). Superiors themselves could be affected by this disease, when they court their collaborators in order to obtain their submission, loyalty and psychological dependency, but the end result is a real complicity.

11. The disease of indifference to others. This is where each individual thinks only of himself and loses sincerity and warmth of human relationships. When the most knowledgeable person does not put that knowledge at the service of his less knowledgeable colleagues. When we learn something and then keep it to ourselves rather than sharing it in a helpful way with others. When out of jealousy or deceit we take joy in seeing others fall instead of helping them up and encouraging them.

12. The disease of a lugubrious face. Those glum and dour persons who think that to be serious we have to put on a face of melancholy and severity, and treat others—especially those we consider our inferiors—with rigor, brusqueness and arrogance. In fact, *a show of severity* and *sterile pessimism*[12] are frequently symptoms of fear and insecurity. An apostle must make an effort to be courteous, serene, enthusiastic and joyful, a person who transmits joy everywhere he goes. A heart filled with God is a happy heart which radiates an infectious joy: it is immediately evident! So let us not lose that joyful, humorous and even self-deprecating spirit which makes people amiable even in difficult situations.[13] How beneficial is a good dose of humor! We would do well to recite often the prayer of St. Thomas More.[14] I say it every day, and it helps.

13. The disease of hoarding. When an apostle tries to fill an existential void in his heart by accumulating material goods, not out of need but only in order to feel secure. The fact is that we are not able to bring material goods with us, since *"the winding sheet does not have pockets,"* and all our earthly treasures—even if they are gifts—will never be able to fill that void; instead, they will only make it deeper and more demanding. To these persons the Lord repeats: *"You say, I am rich, I have prospered and I need nothing; not knowing that you are wretched, pitiable, poor, blind and naked. So be zealous and repent"* (Rev 3:17, 19). Accumulating goods only burdens and inexorably slows down the journey! Here I think of an

---

12   Ibid., nos. 84-86.

13   Ibid., no. 2.

14   "Grant me, O Lord, good digestion, and also something to digest. Grant me a healthy body, and the necessary good humor to maintain it. Grant me a simple soul that knows to treasure all that is good and that doesn't frighten easily at the sight of evil, but rather finds the means to put things back in their place. Give me a soul that knows not boredom, grumbling, sighs and laments, nor excess of stress, because of that obstructing thing called 'I.' Grant me, O Lord, a sense of good humor. Allow me the grace to be able to take a joke and to discover in life a bit of joy, and to be able to share it with others."

anecdote: the Spanish Jesuits used to describe the Society of Jesus as the *"light brigade of the Church."* I remember when a young Jesuit was moving, and while he was loading a truck full of his many possessions, suitcases, books, objects and gifts, an old Jesuit standing by was heard to say with a smile: *And this is "the light brigade of the Church?"* Our moving can be a sign of this disease.

14. The disease of closed circles, where belonging to a clique becomes more powerful than belonging to the Body and, in some circumstances, to Christ himself. This disease too always begins with good intentions, but with the passing of time it enslaves its members and becomes a cancer which threatens the harmony of the Body and causes immense evil—scandals—especially to our weaker brothers and sisters. Self-destruction, *"friendly fire"* from our fellow soldiers, is the most insidious danger.[15] It is the evil which strikes from within;[16] and, as Christ says. "Every kingdom divided against itself is laid waste" (Lk 11:17).

15. Lastly: the disease of worldly profit, of forms of self-exhibition.[17] When an apostle turns his service into power, and his power into a commodity in order to gain worldly profit or even greater power. This is the disease of persons who insatiably try to accumulate power and to this end are ready to slander, defame and discredit others, even in newspapers and magazines. Naturally, so as to put themselves on display and to show that they are more capable than others. This disease does great harm to the Body because it leads persons to justify the use of any means whatsoever to attain their goal, often in the name of justice and transparency! Here I remember a priest who used to call journalists to tell— and invent—private and confidential matters involving his confrères and parishioners. The only thing he was concerned about was being able to see himself on the front page, since this made him feel *"powerful and glamorous,"* while causing great harm to others and to the Church. Poor sad soul!

Brothers, these diseases and these temptations are naturally a danger for each Christian and for every curia, community, congregation, parish

---

15   *Evangelii Gaudium*, no. 88.

16   Bl. Paul VI, referring to the situation of the Church stated that he had the feeling that "through some crack, the smoke of Satan has entered the temple of God": Homily for the Solemnity of Sts. Peter and Paul (June 29, 1972); cf. *Evangelii Gaudium*, nos. 98-101.

17   Cf. *Evangelii Gaudium*, nos. 93-97.

and ecclesial movement; and they can strike at the individual and the community levels.

We need to be clear that it is only the Holy Spirit who can heal all our infirmities. He is the soul of the Mystical Body of Christ; as the Nicene-Constantinopolitan Creed says: "I believe in the Holy Spirit, Lord and *Giver of Life.*" It is the Holy Spirit who sustains every sincere effort at purification and in every effort at conversion. It is he who makes us realize that every member participates in the sanctification of the Body and its weakening. He is the promoter of harmony:[18] "*Ipse harmonia est,*" as St. Basil says. St. Augustine tells us that "as long as a member is still part of the body, its healing can be hoped for. But once it is removed, it can be neither cured nor healed."[19]

Healing also comes about through an awareness of our sickness and of a personal and communal decision to be cured by patiently and perseveringly accepting the remedy.[20]

And so we are called—in this Christmas season and throughout our time of service and our lives—to live "*in truth and love, we must grow up in every way into him who is the head, into Christ, from whom the whole body, joined and knit together by every ligament with which it is equipped, as each part is working properly, promotes the body's growth in building itself up in love*" (Eph 4:15-16).

Dear brothers!

I read once that priests are like planes: they only make news when they crash, even though so many of them are in the air. Many people criticize, and few pray for them. It is a very touching, but also very true saying, because it points to the importance and the frailty of our priestly service, and how much evil a single priest who "crashes" can do to the whole body of the Church.

Therefore, so as not to fall in these days when we are preparing ourselves for Confession, let us ask the Virgin Mary, Mother of God and Mother of the Church, to heal the wounds of sin which each of us bears

---

18   "The Holy Spirit is the soul of the Church. He gives life, he brings forth different charisms which enrich the people of God and, above all, he creates unity among believers: from the many he makes one body, the Body of Christ. . . . The Holy Spirit brings unity to the Church: unity in faith, unity in love, unity in interior cohesion" (Homily at Holy Mass in Turkey, November 29, 2014).

19   Augustine, *Sermo* CXXXVII, 1 (PL 38, 754).

20   Cf. *Evangelii Gaudium*, nos. 25-33.

in his heart, and to sustain the Church and the Curia so that they can be healthy and health-giving; holy and sanctifying, to the glory of her Son and for our salvation and that of the entire world. Let us ask her to make us love the Church as Christ, her Son and our Lord, loves her, to have the courage to acknowledge that we are sinners in need of his mercy, and not to fear surrendering our hands into her maternal hands.

I offer cordial good wishes for a holy Christmas to all of you, to your families and your coworkers. And please, do not forget to pray for me! Heartfelt thanks!

A Catalog of Virtue

Clementine Hall, December 21, 2015

Dear brothers and sisters,

Forgive me for not standing up as I speak to you, but for some days I've been suffering from a cold and not feeling too well. With your permission, I'll speak to you sitting down.

I am pleased to offer heartfelt good wishes for a blessed Christmas and a happy New Year to you and your coworkers, to the Papal Representatives, and in particular to those who in the past year have completed their service and retired. Let us also remember all those who have gone home to God. My thoughts and my gratitude go to you and to the members of your families.

In our meeting in 2013, I wanted to stress two important and inseparable aspects of the work of the Curia: *professionalism and service*, and I offered St. Joseph as a model to be imitated. Then, last year, as a preparation for the sacrament of Reconciliation, we spoke of certain temptations or maladies—the *catalogue of curial diseases*; today instead I would like to speak about "curial antibiotics"—which could affect any Christian, curia, community, congregation, parish or ecclesial movement. Diseases which call for prevention, vigilance, care and, sadly, in some cases, painful and prolonged interventions.

Some of these diseases became evident in the course of the past year, causing no small pain to the entire body and harming many souls, even by scandal.

It seems necessary to state what has been—and ever shall be—the object of sincere reflection and decisive provisions. The reform will move forward with determination, clarity and firm resolve, since *Ecclesia semper reformanda*.

Nonetheless, diseases and even scandals cannot obscure the efficiency of the services rendered to the Pope and to the entire Church by the Roman Curia, with great effort, responsibility, commitment and dedication, and this is a real source of consolation. St. Ignatius taught that "it is typical of the evil spirit to instill remorse, sadness and difficulties, and to cause needless worry so as to prevent us from going forward; instead, it is typical of the good spirit to instill courage and energy, consolations and tears, inspirations and serenity, and to lessen and remove every difficulty so as to make us advance on the path of goodness."[21]

It would be a grave injustice not to express heartfelt gratitude and needed encouragement to all those good and honest men and women in the Curia who work with dedication, devotion, fidelity and professionalism, offering to the Church and the Successor of Peter the assurance of their solidarity and obedience, as well as their constant prayers.

Moreover, cases of resistance, difficulties and failures on the part of individuals and ministers are so many lessons and opportunities for growth, and never for discouragement. They are opportunities for *returning to the essentials*, which means being ever more conscious of ourselves, of God and our neighbors, of the *sensus Ecclesiae* and the *sensus fidei*.

It is about this *return to essentials* that I wish to speak today, just a few days after the Church's inauguration of the pilgrimage of the Holy Year of Mercy, a Year which represents for her and for all of us a pressing summons to *gratitude, conversion, renewal, penance* and *reconciliation*.

Christmas is truly the feast of God's infinite mercy, as St. Augustine of Hippo tells us: "*Could there have been any greater mercy shown to us unhappy men than that which led the Creator of the heavens to come down among us, and the Creator of the earth to take on our mortal body? That same mercy led the Lord of the world to assume the nature of a servant, so that, being himself bread, he would suffer hunger; being himself satiety, he would thirst; being himself power, he would know weakness; being himself salvation, he would experience our woundedness, and being himself life, he would die. All this he did to assuage our hunger, alleviate our longing, strengthen our weaknesses, wipe out our sins and enkindle our charity.*"[22]

Consequently, in the context of this Year of Mercy and our own preparation for the coming celebration of Christmas, I would like to present a practical aid for fruitfully experiencing this season of grace. It is by no means an exhaustive *catalogue of needed virtues* for those who serve in the Curia and for all those who would like to make their consecration or service to the Church more fruitful.

---

21   *Spiritual Exercises*, 315.

22   Cf. *Sermo* CCVII, 1 (PL 38, 1042).

I would ask the Heads of Dicasteries and other superiors to ponder this, to add to it and to complete it. It is a list based on an acrostic analysis of the word **Misericordia**—Fr. Ricci did this in China—with the aim of having it serve as our guide and beacon:

1. **M**issionary and pastoral spirit: missionary spirit is what makes the Curia evidently fertile and fruitful; it is proof of the effectiveness, efficiency and authenticity of our activity. Faith is a gift, yet the measure of our faith is also seen by the extent to which we communicate it.[23] All baptized persons are missionaries of the Good News, above all by their lives, their work and their witness of joy and conviction. A sound pastoral spirit is an indispensable virtue for the priest in particular. It is shown in his daily effort to follow the Good Shepherd who cares for the flock and gives his life to save the lives of others. It is the yardstick for our curial and priestly work. Without these two wings we could never take flight, or even enjoy the happiness of the "faithful servant" (Mt 25:14-30).

2. **I**doneity and sagacity: idoneity, or suitability, entails personal effort aimed at acquiring the necessary requisites for exercising as best we can our tasks and duties with intelligence and insight. It does not countenance "recommendations" and payoffs. Sagacity is the readiness to grasp and confront situations with shrewdness and creativity. Idoneity and sagacity also represent our human response to divine grace, when we let ourselves follow the famous dictum: "Do everything as if God did not exist and then put it all in God's hands as if you did not exist." It is the approach of the disciple who prays to the Lord every day in the words of the beautiful Universal Prayer attributed to Pope Clement XI: "Vouchsafe to conduct me by your wisdom, to restrain me by your justice, to comfort me by your mercy, to defend me by your power. To thee I desire to consecrate all my thoughts, words, actions and sufferings; that henceforth I may think only of you, speak of you, refer all my actions to your greater glory, and suffer willingly whatever you appoint."[24]

---

23 "Missionary spirit is not only about geographical territories, but about peoples, cultures and individuals, because the "boundaries" of faith do not only cross places and human traditions, but the heart of each man and each woman. The Second Vatican Council emphasized in a special way how the missionary task, that of broadening the boundaries of faith, belongs to every baptized person and all Christian communities," Message for World Mission Day 2013, no. 2.

24 *Missale Romanum* (2002).

3. **S**pirituality and humanity: spirituality is the backbone of all service in the Church and in the Christian life. It is what nourishes all our activity, sustaining and protecting it from human frailty and daily temptation. Humanity is what embodies the truthfulness of our faith; those who renounce their humanity renounce everything. Humanity is what makes us different from machines and robots which feel nothing and are never moved. Once we find it hard to weep seriously or to laugh heartily —these are just two signs—we have begun our decline and the process of turning from "humans" into something else. Humanity is knowing how to show tenderness and fidelity and courtesy to all (cf. Phil 4:5). Spirituality and humanity, while innate qualities, are a potential needing to be activated fully, attained completely and demonstrated daily.

4. **E**xample and fidelity: Blessed Paul VI reminded the Curia—in 1963—of "its calling to set an example."[23] An example of avoiding scandals which harm souls and impair the credibility of our witness. Fidelity to our consecration, to our vocation, always mindful of the words of Christ, "Whoever is faithful in a very little is faithful also in much; and whoever is dishonest in a very little is dishonest also in much" (Lk 16:10) and, "If any of you put a stumbling block before one of these little ones who believe in me, it would be better for you if a great millstone were fastened around your neck and you were drowned in the depth of the sea. Woe to the world for stumbling blocks! Occasions for stumbling are bound to come, but woe to the one by whom the stumbling block comes" (Mt 18:6-7).

5. **R**easonableness and gentleness: reasonableness helps avoid emotional excesses, while gentleness helps avoid an excess of bureaucracy, programs and planning. These qualities are necessary for a balanced personality: "The enemy"—and forgive me for quoting St. Ignatius once again—"pays careful heed to whether a soul is coarse or delicate; if it is delicate, he finds a way to make it overly delicate, in order to cause it greater distress and confusion."[26] Every excess is a symptom of some imbalance, be it an excess of reasoning or of delicateness.

6. **I**nnocuousness and determination: innocuousness makes us cautious in our judgments and capable of refraining from impulsive and hasty actions. It is the ability to bring out the best in ourselves, in others

25   Pope Paul VI, Address to the Roman Curia (September 21, 1963): AAS 55 (1963), 793-800.

26   *Spiritual Exercises*, 349.

and in all kinds of situations by acting carefully and attentively. It consists of doing unto others what we would have them do to us (cf. Mt 7:12 and Lk 6:31). Determination is acting with a resolute will, clear vision, obedience to God and solely for the supreme law of the *salus animarum* (cf. CIC, c. 1725).

7. **C**harity and truth: two inseparable virtues of the Christian life, "speaking the truth in charity and practicing charity in truth" (cf. Eph 4:15).[27] To the point where charity without truth becomes a destructive ideology of complaisance and truth without charity becomes myopic legalism.

8. **O**penness and maturity: openness is honesty and rectitude, consistency and absolute sincerity with regard both to ourselves and to God. An honest and open person does not act virtuously only when he or she is being watched; honest persons have no fear of being caught, since they never betray the trust of others. An honest person is never domineering like the "wicked servant" (cf. Mt 24:48-51), with regard to the persons or matters entrusted to his or her care. Honesty is the foundation on which all other qualities rest. Maturity is the quest to achieve balance and harmony in our physical, mental and spiritual gifts. It is the goal and outcome of a never-ending process of development which has nothing to do with age.

9. **R**espectfulness and humility: respectfulness is an endowment of those noble and tactful souls who always try to show genuine respect for others, for their own work, for their superiors and subordinates, for dossiers and papers, for confidentiality and privacy, who can listen carefully and speak politely. Humility is the virtue of the saints and those godly persons who become all the more important as they come to realize that they are nothing, and can do nothing, apart from God's grace (cf. Jn 15:8).

10. **D**iligence and attentiveness: the more we trust in God and his providence, the more we grow in diligence and readiness to give of

---

27   "Charity in truth, to which Jesus Christ bore witness by his earthly life and especially by his death and resurrection, is the principal driving force behind the authentic development of every person and of all humanity. . . . It is a force that has its origin in God, Eternal Love and Absolute Truth" (Benedict XVI, Encyclical Letter *Caritas in Veritate* [June 29, 2009], no. 1: AAS 101 (2009), 641); hence the need to "link charity with truth not only in the sequence, pointed out by St. Paul, of *veritas in caritate* (Eph 4:15), but also in the inverse and complementary sequence of *caritas in veritate*. Truth needs to be sought, found and expressed within the 'economy' of charity, but charity in its turn needs to be understood, confirmed and practiced in the light of truth" (ibid., no. 2).

ourselves, in the knowledge that the more we give the more we receive. What good would it do to open all the Holy Doors of all the basilicas in the world if the doors of our own heart are closed to love, if our hands are closed to giving, if our homes are closed to hospitality and our churches to welcome and acceptance. Attentiveness is concern for the little things, for doing our best and never yielding to our vices and failings. St. Vincent de Paul used to pray: "Lord, help me to be always aware of those around me, those who are worried or dismayed, those suffering in silence, and those who feel alone and abandoned."

11. **I**ntrepidness and alertness: being intrepid means fearlessness in the face of troubles, like Daniel in the den of lions, or David before Goliath. It means acting with boldness, determination and resolve, "as a good soldier" (2 Tm 2:3-4). It means being immediately ready to take the first step, like Abraham, or Mary. Alertness, on the other hand, is the ability to act freely and easily, without being attached to fleeting material things. The Psalm says: "If riches increase, set not your heart on them" (Ps 61:10). To be alert means to be always on the go, and never being burdened by the accumulation of needless things, caught up in our own concerns and driven by ambition.

12. **A**ccountability and sobriety, finally: accountable and trustworthy persons are those who honor their commitments with seriousness and responsibility when they are being observed, but above all when they are alone; they radiate a sense of tranquility because they never betray a trust. Sobriety—the last virtue on this list, but not because it is least important—is the ability to renounce what is superfluous and to resist the dominant consumerist mentality. Sobriety is prudence, simplicity, straightforwardness, balance and temperance. Sobriety is seeing the world through God's eyes and from the side of the poor. Sobriety is a style of life[28] which points to the primacy of others as a hierarchical principle and is shown in a life of concern and service toward others. The sober person is consistent and straightforward in all things, because he or she can reduce, recover, recycle, repair, and live a life of moderation.

---

28   A style of life marked by sobriety restores "that disinterested, unselfish and aesthetic attitude that is born of wonder in the presence of being and of the beauty which enables one to see in visible things the message of the invisible God who created them" (John Paul II, Encyclical *Centesimus Annus* [May 1, 1991], no. 37); cf. AA.VV, *Nuovi stili di vita nel tempo della globalizzazione*, Fondazione Apostolicam Actuositatem, Rome, 2002.

Dear brothers and sisters,

Mercy is no fleeting sentiment, but rather the synthesis of the joyful Good News, a choice and decision on the part of all who desire to put on the "Heart of Jesus"[29] and to be serious followers of the Lord who has asked us to "be merciful even as your heavenly Father is merciful" (Mt 5:48; Lk 6:36). In the words of Fr. Ermes Ronchi, "Mercy is a scandal for justice, a folly for intelligence, a consolation for us who are debtors. The debt for being alive, the debt for being loved is only repayable by mercy."

And so may mercy guide our steps, inspire our reforms and enlighten our decisions. May it be the basis of all our efforts. May it teach us when to move forward and when to step back. May it also enable us to understand the littleness of all that we do in God's greater plan of salvation and his majestic and mysterious working.

To help us better grasp this, let us savor the magnificent prayer, commonly attributed to Bl. Oscar Arnulfo Romero, but pronounced for the first time by Cardinal John Dearden:

Every now and then it helps us to take a step back
and to see things from a distance.
The Kingdom is not only beyond our efforts, it is also
    beyond our visions.
In our lives, we manage to achieve only a small part
of the marvelous plan that is God's work.
Nothing that we do is complete,
which is to say that the Kingdom is greater than ourselves.
No statement says everything that can be said.
No prayer completely expresses the faith.
No Creed brings perfection.
No pastoral visit solves every problem.
No program fully accomplishes the mission of the Church.
No goal or purpose ever reaches completion.

---

29   St. John Paul II, *Angelus* (July 9, 1989): "The expression 'Heart of Jesus' immediately calls to mind Christ's humanity and emphasizes the wealth of his feelings: his compassion for the sick; his predilection for the poor; his mercy for sinners; his tenderness toward children; his strength in denouncing the hypocrisy of pride and violence; his meekness before his opponents; his zeal for the glory of the Father, and his rejoicing in the mysterious and providential plans of his grace. . . . [It] recalls Christ's sorrow over his betrayal by Judas, his distress due to loneliness, his anguish in the face of death, his filial and obedient abandonment into the hands of the Father. Most of all, it speaks of the love which flows unceasingly from his inmost being: infinite love for the Father and limitless love for mankind."

This is what it is about:
We plant seeds that one day will grow.
We water seeds already planted,
knowing that others will watch over them.
We lay the foundations of something that will develop.
We add the yeast which will multiply our possibilities.
We cannot do everything,
yet it is liberating to begin.
This gives us the strength to do something and to do it well.
It may remain incomplete, but it is a beginning, a step
    along the way.
It is an opportunity for the grace of God to enter
and to do the rest.
It may be that we will never see its completion,
but that is the difference between the master and the laborer.
We are laborers, not master builders,
servants, not the Messiah.
We are prophets of a future that does not belong to us.

And with these thoughts and sentiments, I wish you a happy and
holy Christmas, and I ask you to pray for me. Thank you.

Other Occasions

This Is How the Lord Is

Mass in the Chapel of Casa Santa Maria

May 17, 2013

I once knew of a priest, a good parish pastor who worked well. He was appointed bishop, and he was ashamed because he did not feel worthy, he had a spiritual torment. And he went to the confessor. The confessor heard him and said, "But do not worry. If after the [mess Peter made of things], they made him Pope, then you go ahead!" The point is that this is how the Lord is. That's the way He is. The Lord makes us mature with many meetings with Him, even with our weaknesses, when we recognize [them], with our sins. That is how he is, and the story of Peter who let himself be shaped—I think that is how you say it—by his many encounters with Jesus, is for all of us, because we are on the same road behind Jesus to practice the Gospel. Peter is great, but not because he is a doctor of this or because he is a good man that did this. No, he is a great man, because he has a nobility of heart, which brings him to tears, leads him to this pain, this shame and also to take up his work of shepherding the flock.

Today the Bishop Has Come

Visit to the Roman Parish of Sts. Elizabeth and Zechariah

May 26, 2013

I thank you too for your welcome on this day of the Feast of the Trinity. There are priests here whom you know well, the two secretaries of the Pope, the Pope who is in the Vatican, isn't he? Today the Bishop of Rome has come here. And these two work hard. But today one of them, Fr. Alfred, is celebrating the anniversary of his priestly ordination: twenty-nine years. Give him a round of applause! Let us pray for him and ask for at least another twenty-nine years for him. Shall we? Let us begin Mass like this, with a spirit of devotion, in silence, all praying together for all of us.

A Special Remembrance

Angelus, *August 4, 2013*

I would like to assure you of my special remembrance for parish priests and for all the priests in the world because today we are commemorating their Patron, St. John Mary Vianney. Dear confreres, let us be united in prayer and in pastoral charity.

When Priests Don't Make the News

Mass in the Chapel of Casa Santa Marta

January 27, 2014

Bishops are not chosen merely to carry forward an organization called a particular Church. They are anointed. They have the anointing and the Spirit of the Lord is with them. We bishops are all sinners, but we are anointed! We all want to be holier each day, we want to be more faithful to this anointing. And what makes the Church, what gives unity to the Church is the person of the bishop, in the name of Jesus Christ, because he has been anointed: not because he has a majority vote, but because he is anointed.

The particular Church derives its strength from this anointing and, through participation, priests are also anointed: the bishops lay hands and effect this anointing in them. The priests carry forward parishes and many other works. For bishops and priests, this anointing is their strength and their joy. . . .

When we think of bishops, of priests—both are priests because this is the priesthood of Christ: bishop and priest—we should think of them in this way: as anointed. Otherwise, we cannot understand the Church. Not only would we not understand her but we would also be unable to explain how the Church continues on only by human strength. A diocese moves forward because its people are holy . . . and because one who is anointed helps it to grow. The same is true for a parish, which carries on because it has many organizations . . . but also because it has a priest: an anointed one who leads it forward.

We only remember a small handful of the many holy bishops, the many priests, the many holy priests who have dedicated their entire lives to the service of the diocese, of the parish. . . . Parish priests in the countryside and parish priests in the city who by their anointing gave their people strength, transmitted doctrine, conferred the sacraments; that is, holiness.

Someone might object: "But, Father, I read in the newspaper that a bishop did such, or that a priest did such and such!" Yes, I read it too!

But tell me: Do the newspapers print all the good that so many priests do, so many priests in so many parishes in the city and countryside? The charity they show? The work they do to carry their people forward? "No, this isn't news!" A single tree falling in the forest causes more sound than an entire forest that slowly grows and matures.

Those Who Scandalize the People

Mass in the Chapel of Casa Santa Maria

Once, newly ordained, I was with a group from the university and a couple who wanted to get married. They went to a parish to arrange the wedding mass. And the parish secretary there, said: "No, no, you can't." And they asked why they couldn't have a wedding mass, since a Mass was always recommended in order to marry. "No, it's not possible, because you can't take more than twenty minutes." Why? "Because there are time slots"—But we want a Mass!—"Then pay for two slots!" So, in order to marry with a Mass they had to pay twice." This is a scandal. And we know what Jesus says to those who cause scandal: it would be better to be cast into the sea.

When those who are in the temple—whether priests, lay people, secretaries who manage pastoral care in the temple—become profiteers, the people will be scandalized. And all of us, the laity as well, are responsible for this. Because, if I see this going on in my parish, I have to have the courage to speak to the priest's face, otherwise, the people suffer that scandal. And it's curious that the People of God lose their priests, when they have a weakness, slipping on a sin. However, there are two things that the People of God cannot forgive: a priest attached to money and a priest who mistreats people. That is hard to forgive. . . .

Why does Jesus have an issue with money? Because, redemption is free: God's gratuitousness. Jesus comes to bring us the full gratuitousness of the love of God. When the Church or the churches become profiteers, it's said that salvation isn't so free. It is for this very reason that Jesus takes the lash in hand to do this rite of purification in the temple (cf. Lk 19:45-48).

Meeting with Victims of Sexual Abuse

St. Charles Borromeo Seminary

Philadelphia, September 27, 2015

My dearest brothers and sisters in Christ, I am grateful for this opportunity to meet you, I am blessed by your presence. Thank you for coming here today.

Words cannot fully express my sorrow for the abuse you suffered. You are precious children of God who should always expect our protection, our care and our love. I am profoundly sorry that your innocence was violated by those who you trusted. In some cases the trust was betrayed by members of your own family, in other cases by priests who carry a sacred responsibility for the care of soul. In all circumstances, the betrayal was a terrible violation of human dignity.

For those who were abused by a member of the clergy, I am deeply sorry for the times when you or your family spoke out, to report the abuse, but you were not heard or believed. Please know that the Holy Father hears you and believes you. I deeply regret that some bishops failed in their responsibility to protect children. It is very disturbing to know that in some cases bishops even were abusers. I pledge to you that we will follow the path of truth wherever it may lead. Clergy and bishops will be held accountable when they abuse or fail to protect children.

We are gathered here in Philadelphia to celebrate God's gift of family life. Within our family of faith and our human families, the sins and crimes of sexual abuse of children must no longer be held in secret and in shame. As we anticipate the Jubilee Year of Mercy, your presence, so generously given despite the anger and pain you have experienced, reveals the merciful heart of Christ. Your stories of survival, each unique and compelling, are powerful signs of the hope that comes from the Lord's promise to be with us always.

It is good to know that you have brought family members and friends with you today. I am grateful for their compassionate support and pray that many people of the Church will respond to the call to accompany those who have suffered abuse. May the Door of Mercy be opened wide in our dioceses, our parishes, our homes and our hearts, to receive those who were abused and to seek the path to forgiveness by trusting in the Lord. We promise to support your continued healing and to always be vigilant to protect the children of today and tomorrow.

When the disciples who walked with Jesus on the road to Emmaus recognized that He was the Risen Lord, they asked Jesus to stay with them. Like those disciples, I humbly beg you and all survivors of abuse to stay with us, to stay with the Church, and that together, as pilgrims on the journey of faith, we might find our way to the Father.

Jubilee of Mercy for Priests

Mass in St. Peter's Square

Solemnity of the Most Sacred Heart of Jesus, June 3, 2016

This celebration of the Jubilee for Priests on the Solemnity of the Sacred Heart of Jesus invites us all to turn to the heart, the deepest root and foundation of every person, the focus of our affective life and, in a word, his or her very core. Today we contemplate two hearts: the *Heart of the Good Shepherd* and *our own heart as priests*.

The Heart of the Good Shepherd is not only the Heart that shows us mercy, but *is* itself mercy. There the Father's love shines forth; there I know I am welcomed and understood as I am; there, with all my sins and limitations, I know the certainty that I am chosen and loved. Contemplating that heart, I renew my first love: the memory of that time when the Lord touched my soul and called me to follow him, the memory of the joy of having cast the nets of our life upon the sea of his word (cf. Lk 5:5).

The Heart of the Good Shepherd tells us that his love is limitless; it is never exhausted and it never gives up. There we see his infinite and boundless self-giving; there we find the source of that faithful and meek love which sets free and makes others free; there we constantly discover anew that Jesus loves us "even to the end" (Jn 13:1), to the very end, without ever imposing.

The Heart of the Good Shepherd reaches out to us, above all to those who are most distant. There the needle of his compass inevitably points, there we see a particular "weakness" of his love, which desires to embrace all and lose none.

Contemplating the Heart of Christ, we are faced with the fundamental question of our priestly life: *Where is my heart directed?* It is a question we need to keep asking, daily, weekly . . . *Where is my heart directed?* Our ministry is often full of plans, projects and activities: from catechesis to liturgy, to works of charity, to pastoral and administrative commitments. Amid all these, we must still ask ourselves: What is my heart set on? I think of that beautiful prayer of the liturgy, "*Ubi vera sunt gaudia*" . . . Where is it directed, what is the treasure that it seeks? For as Jesus says: "Where your treasure is, there will your heart be also" (Mt 6:21). All of us have our weaknesses and sins. But let us go deeper: what is the root of our failings, those sins, the place we have hid that "treasure" that keeps us from the Lord?

The great riches of the Heart of Jesus are two: the Father and ourselves. His days were divided between prayer to the Father and encountering people. Not distance, but encounter. So too the heart of Christ's priests knows only two directions: *the Lord and his people*. The heart of the priest is a heart pierced by the love of the Lord. For this reason, he no longer looks to himself, or should look to himself, but is instead turned toward God and his brothers and sisters. It is no longer "a fluttering heart," allured by momentary whims, shunning disagreements and seeking petty satisfactions. Rather, it is a heart rooted firmly in the Lord, warmed by the Holy Spirit, open and available to our brothers and sisters. That is where our sins are resolved.

To help our hearts burn with the charity of Jesus the Good Shepherd, we can train ourselves to do three things suggested to us by today's readings: *seek out*, *include* and *rejoice*.

Seek out. The prophet Ezekiel reminds us that God himself goes out in search of his sheep (Ez 34:11, 16). As the Gospel says, he "goes out in search of the one who is lost" (Lk 15:4), without fear of the risks. Without delaying, he leaves the pasture and his regular workday. He doesn't demand overtime. He does not put off the search. He does not think: "I have done enough for today; perhaps I'll worry about it tomorrow". Instead, he immediately sets to it; his heart is anxious until he finds that one lost sheep. Having found it, he forgets his weariness and puts the sheep on his shoulders, fully content. Sometimes he has to go and seek it out, to speak, to persuade; at other times he must remain in prayer before the tabernacle, struggling with the Lord for that sheep.

Such is a heart that seeks out. A heart that does not set aside times and spaces as private. Woe to those shepherds to privatize their ministry! It is not jealous of its legitimate quiet time, even that, and never demands that it be left alone. A shepherd after the heart of God does not protect his own comfort zone. He is not worried about protecting his good name, but will be slandered as Jesus was. Unafraid of criticism, he is disposed to take risks in seeking to imitate his Lord. "Blessed are you when people revile you and persecute you. . . ." (Mt 5:11).

A shepherd after the heart of God has a heart sufficiently free to set aside his own concerns. He does not live by calculating his gains or how long he has worked: he is not an accountant of the Spirit, but a Good Samaritan who seeks out those in need. For the flock he is a shepherd, not an inspector, and he devotes himself to the mission not fifty or sixty percent, but with all he has. In seeking, he finds, and he finds because he takes risks. Unless a shepherd risks, he does not find. He does not stop when disappointed and he does not yield to weariness. Indeed, he is *stubborn in doing good*, anointed with the divine obstinacy that loses sight of no one. Not only does he keep his doors open, but he also goes to seek out those who no longer wish to enter them. Like every good Christian, and as an example for every Christian, he constantly *goes out of himself*. The epicenter of his heart is outside of himself. He is centered only in Jesus, not in himself. He is not attracted by his own "I," but by the "Thou" of God and by the "we" of other men and women.

The second word: *Include*. Christ loves and knows his sheep. He gives his life for them, and no one is a stranger to him (cf. Jn 10:11-14). His flock is his family and his life. He is not a boss to be feared by his flock, but a shepherd who walks alongside them and calls them by name (cf. Jn 10:3-4). He wants to gather the sheep that are not yet of his fold (cf. Jn 10:16).

So it is also with the priest of Christ. He is anointed for his people, not to choose his own projects but to be close to the real men and women whom God has entrusted to him. No one is excluded from his heart, his prayers or his smile. With a father's loving gaze and heart, he welcomes and includes everyone, and if at times he has to correct, it is to draw people closer. He stands apart from no one, but is always ready to dirty his hands. The Good Shepherd does not wear gloves. As a minister of the communion that he celebrates and lives, he does not await greetings and compliments from others, but is the first to reach out, rejecting gossip, judgements and malice. He listens patiently to the problems of his people and accompanies them, sowing God's forgiveness with generous compassion. He does not scold those who wander off or lose their way, but is always ready to bring them back and to resolve difficulties and disagreements. He knows how to *include*.

Rejoice. God is "full of joy" (cf. Lk 15:5). His joy is born of forgiveness, of life risen and renewed, of prodigal children who breathe once more the sweet air of home. The joy of Jesus the Good Shepherd is not a joy *for himself* alone, but a joy *for others and with others*, the true joy of love. This is also the joy of the priest. He is changed by the mercy that he *freely* gives. In prayer he discovers God's consolation and realizes that nothing is more powerful than his love. He thus experiences inner peace, and is happy to be a channel of mercy, to bring men and women closer to the Heart of God. Sadness for him is not the norm, but only a step along the way; harshness is foreign to him, because he is a shepherd after the meek Heart of God.

Dear priests, in the Eucharistic celebration we rediscover each day our identity as shepherds. In every Mass, may we truly make our own Christ's words: "This is my body, which is given up for you." This is the meaning of our life; with these words, in a real way we can daily renew the promises we made at our priestly ordination. I thank all of you for saying "yes," and also for all those many times you secretly say "yes" each day, things that only the Lord knows about. I thank you for saying "yes" to *giving your life in union with Jesus*: for in this is found the pure source of our joy.